FRANCE
The Crossroads of Europe

by Susan Balerdi

WESTERN BRANCH LIBRARY
611 S. LOMBARDY DRIVE
SOUTH BEND, INDIANA 46619

Dillon Press, Inc.   Minneapolis, Minnesota 55415

For Felix, Matti, Zandy, and Andrew

Library of Congress Cataloging in Publication Data

Balerdi, Susan.
　France, the crossroads of Europe.

　(Discovering our heritage)
　Bibliography: p. 138.
　Includes index.
　Summary: Discusses France's history and geography, languages, foods, folklore, holiday traditions, family and school life, sports, and games, in addition to examining that country's contribution to American life.
　　1. France—Juvenile literature. [1. France]
　I. Title. II. Series.
DC17.B28　　1984　　　944　　　　　83-23198
ISBN 0-87518-248-8

© 1984 by Dillon Press, Inc. All rights reserved

Dillon Press, Inc., 500 South Third Street
Minneapolis, Minnesota 55415

Printed in the United States of America
1　2　3　4　5　6　7　8　9　10　92　91　90　89　88　87　86　85　84

```
j944 B28f      WES
Balerdi, Susan
France, the crossroads of
 Europe
```

Contents

	Fast Facts About France	4
	Map of France	6
1	A Changing Land	7
2	Hyphens, French, and Great Cooking	21
3	The Glory of France	37
4	Of Little People and Tall Tales	59
5	Days to Make Merry	68
6	At Home and in the Kitchen	78
7	School Days	92
8	The French at Play	102
9	From France to America	113
	Appendix A: French Consulates in the United States and Canada	125
	Appendix B: A Note About Pronouncing French Words	127
	Glossary	129
	Selected Bibliography	138
	Index	139

Fast Facts About France

Official Name: *République Française* (French Republic).

Capital: Paris.

Location: Western Europe; France is bordered on the north by Belgium, Luxembourg, and West Germany, on the east by Switzerland and Italy, on the south by Spain, and on the west by the North Atlantic Ocean.

Area: Metropolitan France (mainland and Corsica), 211,208 square miles (547,026 square kilometers); the greatest distance from north to south is 590 miles (950 kilometers) and from east to west 605 miles (974 kilometers). France has 2,300 miles (3,701 kilometers) of coastline.

Elevation: *Highest*—Mont Blanc, 15,771 feet (4,807 meters) above sea level. *Lowest*—below sea level along the delta of the Rhône River.

Population: Metropolitan France, *Estimated 1983 Population*—54,360,000; *Distribution*—78 percent of the people live in or near cities; 22 percent live in rural areas; *Density*—256 persons per square mile (99 persons per square kilometer).

Form of Government: Democratic republic; *Head of State*—president; *Head of Government*—prime minister.

Important Products: Barley, cattle (beef and dairy), corn, grapes, hogs, oats, potatoes, sheep, wheat; cod, crabs, herring, lobsters, mackerel, oysters, sardines, shrimp, tuna; aircraft, aluminum, automobiles, chemicals, iron and steel, perfume, textiles, wine; bauxite, coal, gypsum, iron ore, potash, uranium.
Basic Unit of Money: Franc.
Major Language: French.
Major Religion: Christianity.
Flag: Known as the *tricolore* because of its three vertical stripes, one blue, one white, and one red.
National Anthem: "La Marseillaise."
Major Holidays: New Year's Day—January 1; Epiphany—January 6; Candlemas—February 2; Mardi Gras (Shrove Tuesday)—last Tuesday before the beginning of Lent; Easter Day; Bastille Day—July 14; Christmas Day—December 25.

1. A Changing Land

In many ways France is a very modern country. In other ways it is an old-fashioned one. Old church towers compete with new skyscrapers for control of the clouds. Small landowners farm in the same way that their grandfathers did, but huge nuclear power plants provide over one-third of France's electricity.

Aside from the Soviet Union, France is the largest country in Europe. Let's pretend we could put France onto a map of the United States. It would just about cover the state of Texas.

France also governs several smaller lands called the *territoires d' Outre-Mer,* or "Overseas Territories." They are located in the South Pacific Ocean, Africa, Latin America, and the Caribbean Sea. The closest French territories to the United States are Martinique and Guadeloupe. These islands are only one and a half hours by plane from Miami, Florida.

Like many large nations, France has several different regions, each with its own climate. In mountainous areas you may see children playing in the snow on any day of the year. Yet on the same day in another part of France you may see other children waterskiing.

Mont Pelée is a famous volcano on the island of Martinique, one of France's Overseas Territories.

The people of France differ from one another, too. In the country, some girls and boys get up early to help milk the cows while their friends in the cities are still fast asleep in their cozy beds. Along the coasts, young people may help to catch fish and lobsters.

In the lowlands of north and northeast France, many people work in factories. Here, the cities of Lille, Roubaix, and Tourcoing have grown so much that they have practically become one city.

There are many reasons why the Lille area has become so important. One of them is that Lille is France's traditional textile center. Another is that since the beginning of the twentieth century new

A Changing Land

industries have developed in the area. They include food-processing operations, chemical plants, machine-manufacturing factories, and iron and steel works. Large deposits of certain minerals have also spurred the area's development. Coal and bauxite, the main metal used to make aluminum, are mined in the region. Finally, Lille is very close to the countries France has been doing business with since the end of World War II—West Germany, Belgium, The Netherlands, Denmark, and Luxembourg. Lille is only nine miles from the Belgian border, and very close to Germany and Luxembourg as well.

One of France's richest dairy lands is in the northern part of the country. The province of Normandy is famous for its small, pretty farmhouses, which are built out of stone and have thatched straw roofs. Spotted cattle may often be seen grazing in the open pastures that lie near the farmhouses.

To the west of Normandy, in Brittany, there are three separate kinds of lands. One, an inland area called *le bocage*, or "wooded country," is blanketed by dense oak, maple, and plane-tree forests. Bordering the forests are the Breton farmlands. From any hilltop, you'll see rows of hedges crisscrossing the land, dividing one farm from another. Finally, there is the Breton seashore. Dotted with hundreds of unexplored islands and rocky headlands, it has long been a favorite spot for artists and authors to describe in their own special way.

South of Brittany, Les Landes has the Atlantic Ocean pounding at its sandy shores. For centuries the ocean's winds swept across these shores, blowing the sand inland. The people living here became more and more afraid this erosion would take away their farms. At last, in the eighteenth century, they planted a great pine forest all along the seashore. These pine trees still stand today, protecting the land.

France's central region is called the *bassin de Paris*, or "Parisian Basin." It is a long, flat plain stretching from Paris into the middle of France. For as far as you can see, the land is one wide-open space. You will rarely see trees near the fields, except for those planted as borders along the roads or rivers.

Sunny southern France is bathed and warmed by the Mediterranean Sea. It is also the place where the great Alps and Pyrénées Mountains meet the water. Here you can see many villages over two thousand years old perched on rocky mountaintops. Hillside farmers must grow their crops in fields called terraces—small, thin plots built on different levels in the mountainside. Terracing also keeps the soil from washing away when rain falls.

More and more French people come to live in the warm south every year. The newer towns and villages

The towering Alps Mountains form the border between France and Italy.

they have built are down on the plains. As in Les Landes, many settlers have helped to reclaim France from the sea. In the swamps of Les Camargues, much of this new land is used for growing rice.

The Alps and Pyrénées rise high above these plains. The Alps sprawl from the eastern edge of central France to the Mediterranean Sea. The Pyrénées form a natural border between France and Spain.

Very little rain falls on the warm slopes of the Alps and the Pyrénées in southern France. But the northern Alps and central Pyrénées are usually cold and humid. Their slopes are covered with velvet green dales and pine forests which gradually give way to tall, snow-capped peaks. When we think of the Alps, it is this image we see.

You might think there would be all sorts of big animals prowling about in France's mountains and forests. But the only large animal roaming free in them is the wild boar. Wild horses do run free in the marshlands of Les Camargues, though. These beautiful animals make up one of the largest herds of wild horses left in the world today.

Cattle, sheep, chickens, and hogs are some of the more common animals raised in France. They provide French farmers with nearly two-thirds of their income. The French have also found a special job for

A Changing Land

pigs. They are used to sniff out a rare kind of mushroom called a truffle. Truffles add a delicious flavor to just about any fine meal. In the past, the French have tried to train other animals to find truffles because pigs eat a lot and are expensive to feed. But some of the animals they used ate the truffles before people could pick them up. Others didn't know truffles from stones in the soil. And in the end, none of them seemed to find the mushrooms as quickly as the pigs.

Most French people would like to live in the country to enjoy its beauty. But they don't because it is hard to find well-paying jobs there. As a result, over seventy percent of the French people are crowded into cities.

Paris, the capital of France, is the largest and most industrialized city. One of its most famous industries is fashion. Each year buyers from many different countries come to the city to select new items of clothing that have been created by French designers. The choices they make influence clothing styles everywhere. That is why Paris is also often called the fashion capital of the world.

Like most French cities, Paris is also a town of great charm. Its world-famous museums and splendid parks are unequaled. Paris even has a forest called the *bois de Boulogne*, or "Boulogne Woods."

Around 275,000 works of art are housed in the Louvre, a world famous museum and palace located in Paris.

Almost every French city has pretty squares, and flowers often line main boulevards. Many cities also have statues of famous people and hand-carved fountains. In some cities buildings over five hundred years old have been restored to their former glory. They stand proudly next to office buildings of steel and concrete.

Since most cities and towns date from the Middle Ages, their streets aren't very wide. Many in fact are

The magnificent Eiffel Tower rises 984 feet (296 meters) above the Champs de Mars in Paris.

too narrow for cars to pass through. The size of the streets is one reason why the French ride bicycles and mopeds. Another reason is that gasoline is quite costly.

Some cities, like Dijon, have turned their narrow roads into "walking streets" where no bikes, mopeds, or cars are allowed. These streets are not only great for shoppers and children at play, but they also help to reduce air pollution.

The French take pride in making their cities as handsome as their land. But they know that the one can never replace the other. On weekends, or at vacation time, many of them escape to the country.

In France, as in the rest of Europe, speed limits are posted in kilometers. Similarly, signs showing the way to restaurants, gas stations, hotels, or first-aid care have pictures on them instead of words. Known as international road signs, they are used because so many languages are spoken in Europe. A German person driving through France might not be able to read the signs if they were written in French. But the person can easily understand that a picture of a knife and fork means that he or she will be passing a restaurant soon.

Agriculture is one of France's largest industries. French farmers grow practically all the food the country needs. In addition, they produce large

A Changing Land

amounts of wheat, beet sugar, and dairy goods for export to other countries.

About one-half of all French farms are less than thirty acres, and quite a few are still family owned. But as in the United States, the small farmer is becoming rare. As France grows, its need for more food grows, too. To produce this food, farmers must cultivate more land and use bigger, more up-to-date machinery. The government tries to help the farmers by loaning them money to buy new machines. But many of the small farmers end up selling their land because they cannot successfully compete against larger producers.

The French government has also tried to help other industries become more modern. The new city of Fos-sur-Mer, near Marseille, is a wonderful example of the many large projects it has undertaken. Before the government helped build the city, Fos was not much more than marshes. However, it had a large natural port on the Mediterranean Sea, and government planners thought that a port and industrial center could be built there. That way Fos and Marseille, France's largest southern port, could both attract new trade.

Aside from port activities, Fos has a wide variety of new industries. There are oil refineries, aluminum and steel factories, shipbuilding yards, petrochemical

Marseille's Old Harbor, shown here, is used mainly by pleasure boats. Trading ships dock at a much larger port that lies nearby.

plants, and cement and glass works humming busily for as far as the eye can see. You would need to take several days to visit all the factories, shipyards, and port facilities at Fos-sur-Mer.

The government only helps build large projects after years of study. Since the early 1970s, it has had a policy of developing commerce and industry outside of Paris. There are all sorts of programs to help new businesses get started in poorer areas. These programs are part of a ten-year plan aimed at increasing

As this picture indicates, France is a country where the past, the present, and the future live side by side.

France's national wealth. A second ten-year plan for industrial growth has already been agreed upon by the country's leaders. By the end of the 1980s they hope to have completed a large natural park and high-speed train system, among other projects.

France is a republic with a president, a prime minister, and a Parliament. The president, who is elected for a seven-year term of office, heads the state. The prime minister, who is appointed by the president, oversees the operation of the government. The Parliament is a lawmaking body that has two houses, the Senate and the National Assembly. The men and women who are elected to Parliament vote on policies developed by the president and the prime minister. They are also responsible for making laws concerning such matters as crime, elections, and civil liberties.

You have now had a glance at France today. It is a country where the past, the present, and the future live side by side. Old churches stand near modern skyscrapers; electric trains speed beneath ancient streets; and supersonic planes streak over seemingly ageless fields and mountains.

But what are the French themselves really like? As you have already seen, they love change and new ways. In the next chapter you'll learn that they treasure old ways, too.

2. Hyphens, French, and Great Cooking

Let's imagine I'm a magician who can make people's ideas appear before them. And suppose someone in an audience asked me to bring forth a typical French person. First I'd summon up some soft accordion music. Next I'd add a street paved with cobblestones. Finally I'd snap my fingers and a middle-aged man wearing baggy pants and a beret, and riding a rickety bicycle would appear. Strapped to his bike rack would be a *baguette* (a long loaf of French bread), a round of camembert cheese, and a wine bottle.

By now my audience would no doubt be applauding. They would be sure that this man must live somewhere among France's fifty-four million people. But he is not at all what French people are like. He is a stereotype. That is, he's what the audience thinks a French person should look like.

Some people say the French are great lovers. Others say they like to eat and drink. Still others think the French are very witty. To me, they are the *trait d'union*, or "hyphen," of Europe. For just as a hyphen joins two words, the French unite Europe's people and cultures. Some of them have Germanic ancestors. Others are descended from the ancient

Scandinavians. And a great many can trace their ancestry to people from Belgium, Italy, Poland, or Spain.

Indeed, it's hard to picture two French people with exactly the same background. Today you can still find people living in France who were born in other countries. Some of them did not even speak French when they came. What makes them all French now is that they take special pride in the fact that they are different.

France has always welcomed immigrants. In 1066, William, Duke of Normandy, came from France to conquer England. The Anglo-Saxons who ran from his rule sailed to Brittany in France. This was the province right next to William's own Normandy!

Brittany is located in the northwestern part of France. A region of low, rounded hills and rolling plains, it is haunting in its beauty. The twisted, knotty trees that grow in Brittany are all bent inland because of the prevailing winds. They gust south and east across Brittany, coming from the English Channel in the north and the Atlantic Ocean in the west.

The people who live in Brittany are called Bretons. They are hardworking and have simple tastes. Nowadays all Bretons speak French. But many adults still use Breton, which sounds very much like Welsh.

Traditional Breton costumes are worn only for local holiday celebrations.

Its origins can be traced to the Anglo-Saxons that William chased out of England.

The older women in Brittany still wear *coiffes*, tall, lacy headdresses that come in all shapes and sizes. On market days you can easily spot the coiffes above the crowds. Traditional Breton dresses are worn only for local holidays, among them the *pardons*, yearly visits made to a favorite saint's tomb.

Much of Brittany has the look of another time. The cities of Dinan, Vannes, and Vitré are perfect examples. Most of their buildings, which date from the Middle Ages, are only two stories high. They hover over narrow streets paved in cobblestones. The three cities also have huge stone castles and battered fortresses that remind us of the days of King Arthur.

According to legend, Brittany was the home of Sir Lancelot du Lac, one of Arthur's knights. Morgan le Fay, King Arthur's half-sister, was said to be a native Breton, too.

Jules Verne, a famous writer, was also born in Brittany. Like most of his people, he loved sailing and the sea. He said Breton seascapes inspired him to write *Twenty Thousand Leagues Under the Sea.*

Visitors to Brittany sometimes stop at Carnac. Here they marvel at giant upright stones called menhirs. These stones are very much like the ones at Stonehenge in England.

To the south of Brittany is the province of the Pyrénées. The Pyrénées is filled with many mysteries, the biggest of which is the tall, proud people known as the Basques. They have lived in this mountainous region for thousands of years. Many of them have whitewashed, prim homes with red rooftops.

No one is quite sure where the Basques originally came from. Some scientists say they traveled from

Trim-looking buildings with whitewashed walls and red roofs are characteristic of the Basque region.

the Caucasus Mountains in the Soviet Union because Basque sounds very much like the language spoken there. Other scientists say the Basques came from Japan. The only problem is that the Basques don't look oriental at all. But this idea seems possible since some Basque words have the same sound and meaning as certain Japanese ones. Still other experts tell us that Basques are really descendants of American Indians.

Wherever they came from, Basques are important to France. Always great sailors and adventurers, Basques have traveled to the New World since earliest times. They were the first to plant grapevines in California.

Basques have also been valued as great shepherds for centuries. Their skills are as highly prized in Coeur d'Alène, Idaho, as they are in Guéthary, France. Many legends have developed about the Basque shepherd's call, which sounds like a mix between a Swiss yodel and an Indian war cry. Basques say it has scared away many invaders from their land.

The Basques are known for their great strength and love of sports. The Basque games, which usually take place at the end of spring, are as exciting to watch as to play in. Like Robin Hood and Little John, some men roll logs and wrestle. Others take part in tree-chopping contests.

Hyphens, French, and Great Cooking

The Basques invented the game of jai alai, which they call *pelote*. In the United States this game is played with a wicker basket attached to the arm, but in the Basque country it is played with bare hands. Pelote requires great speed, strength, and skill.

Basques are also respected for their hearty appetites. After the games, there are all sorts of food-eating contests. People gulp down various kinds of meat dishes and fancy desserts in the hope of winning one of these contests.

Let's pretend you're a visitor from another planet. You know nothing about the French, but you'd like to learn. I would tell you that two things distinguish the French from other peoples—their language and their food.

The French take great pride in their mother tongue. They even have a proverb about it—"what is not clear is not French." Over 80 million people around the world speak French as their first language. French has also long been the language used by diplomats—people who represent a country in its dealings with other countries—because it is so clear, orderly, and exact. In fact, French is one of the six official languages used at the United Nations.

In recent years, many English words have become part of the French language. One reason for this development is that science plays an important role in modern life, and English lends itself to scientific expression more easily than French. Another reason is that television, movies, and magazines have made certain English words more familiar to the French.

This mixture of French and English is called *franglais*. Many French people object to it. They think that English words should be kept out of their language to maintain its purity. For that reason, the French government has taken all franglais words out of its official papers.

In a way it's a good thing that the French have been on guard against changes in their language. Their watchfulness has helped them to become quite clever and funny. They love to laugh at themselves and their mistakes.

Nevertheless, the French can be very critical of people who do not speak, write, or behave well. But no matter what they think, they always try to be very polite. Indeed, *la politesse*, which is best termed a code of behavior, heavily influences how they use their language.

For example, there are two ways to say *you* in French. One form, *tu*, is used when the speaker is addressing a family member or a good friend. The other, the polite form *vous*, is always used in addressing strangers or people one doesn't know well. If you are not sure which form to use, it is always best to say

Hyphens, French, and Great Cooking

vous, since saying *tu* to someone you don't know well is considered an insult. French is filled with many hidden meanings like this, and if you're not careful, you can make some very big mistakes.

La politesse also involves observing certain customs. For example, when you go into a store you are expected to say, *"Bonjour, Messieur, Dames,"* which means "Hello ladies and gentlemen." Similarly, when you arrive at or leave from work, you are expected to shake everyone's hand—even if you are a dishwasher and your hands are all soapy! French *gendarmes* ("police") must actually practice shaking hands. They have a book called *Advice from an Old Gendarme to a Young Gendarme* that among other things teaches them just how to shake hands properly.

At times, however, the French can be downright rude. In fact, they are often called the most impolite drivers in Europe. When they are behind the wheel of a car, no one knows who they are, and so they can honk and yell all they like.

As you can see then, their language has much to do with making the French what they are. But food has also played an important role in shaping their character. Indeed, if people are what they eat, the French are rich beyond imagination. For perhaps more than any other people, they regard eating as not just a necessity, but as one of life's great pleasures.

The French eat a very light breakfast. They especially enjoy long sourdough breads with butter and jam. Besides hot chocolate, they also drink steaming *café au lait*, "coffee with milk." Even children drink coffee in France. Their parents will put two or three tablespoons of coffee in a bowl and then fill it up with hot milk.

Lunch is the big meal of the day. It usually consists of tasty meats and vegetables, a salad, and a sweet dessert. Except in the largest cities, it usually lasts about two hours. Even the stores close up at noontime.

The French like to have a late, light dinner. A typical meal would consist of soup and cold meats. Dessert could include some fruit, yogurt, or cheeses. Sunday dinners are especially festive events because friends and family gather to enjoy good food and each other's company.

But the dinner table is used for other things besides eating. It is also a place for people to share their ideas and feelings with each other. Some observers think that the best conversation in a French home takes place at the dinner table. Perhaps this is why people often sit at the table talking long after the dishes have been cleared away.

France is also known for its great wines and cheeses. Most of us not living in France think that everyone there grows grapes for wine. But only one million French people work in the wine industry.

Fine wines are under strict government control by means of controlled place of origin laws *(appellation d'origine contrôlée)*. These laws require the growers to be honest in labeling and bottling their wines. A wine made from grapes grown in Bordeaux, for example, can't be bottled or labeled as having come from Pouilly. The laws protect the growers of fine wines from cheap imitations. They also tell wine buyers that they can trust what the label says.

The most famous wine areas of France are in Aquitaine and Burgundy. Aquitaine, located in southwestern France, is the home of the light red Bordeaux wines. Once known as Guyenne, it is threaded with hundreds of rivers, and the minerals they deposit on the land make the soil very rich. In fact, the Bordeaux region is the largest fine wine area in the world. Wine making has been an important activity there for over 2,000 years.

The dark red wines come from Burgundy. This region, located in eastern France, is very rich in history and culture, too. In fact, Burgundy was once the strongest province in France, and the Burgundians fought and lost several wars against French kings. If they hadn't been defeated, France might be called Burgundy today.

Only one-tenth as much wine is made in Burgundy as in Aquitaine. Yet the region produces some of the most highly praised wines in the world.

The French are very proud of their wines. During the summer, many winegrowers give guided tours of their vineyards and wine cellars. The wine cellars, or *caves*, are basements in large family houses called *châteaux*. If you went into the cellars, you could see ancient wine presses. Imagine, some of these wooden presses are over five hundred years old, and a few are still being used today!

In the late summer, the grapes are harvested. This time is called the season of *vendange*, or "fall harvest." Many students like to gather the grapes for a summer job. Even people from other lands enjoy harvesting grapes in France. It is a terrific experience for anyone who joins in.

During the fall, each wine region has its own *fête de la vigne*, or "wine festival." This event celebrates the success of that year's wine harvest. Many visitors are invited from other European countries and there's lots of dancing, singing, parades, and, of course, eating. These festivals last at least one week, and some can go on for almost two weeks.

Cheese, like wine, is a memorable part of any French feast. There are about three hundred kinds of cheese made in France today. The first cheese was

These vineyards are located in Burgundy, a major wine-producing region in eastern France.

probably made by accident about 11,000 years ago. Most likely, a shepherd had been carrying some milk in his pouch all day. When he tried to drink the milk he found that it had turned into a custardy solid called curd. This curd contained a cloudy sweet liquid called whey. People later learned how to make cheese by separating the curd from the whey.

At Camembert, in Normandy, cheeses are no longer made like curdled milk in a pouch. They are produced by workers in modern buildings. But not all cheeses are made in the same way. The most famous cheese of France is Roquefort cheese. It is aged only in the drafty caverns of the Auvergne Mountains.

How the French eat and drink is an important part of their way of life. So, too, is shopping for food, which is usually done on a daily basis. Everywhere you look there are small family-owned specialty shops. Anywhere in France the lights at the *boulangerie*, or "bread shop," are glowing at 4:00 A.M. By opening time at 6:00 A.M. the aroma of fresh bread greets the early customers.

Then there are the *pâtisseries*, or "bakeries." Some of the most delicious cakes in the world are made in these tiny stores. No one I know can walk by a pâtisserie without at least stopping to look.

Market days are something quite different. In most cities, a large town square is set aside for these

Fruits and vegetables are among the many items sold from open stalls on market days.

days once or twice a week. People hurry there by 6:00 A.M. to set up their stands. Shopkeepers, farmers, or salespeople come to sell food and household goods.

The square fills early with people eager to get a bargain. The sellers stand behind cardboard counters, arguing with buyers about lowering their prices. Eventually a deal is made and happy shoppers scurry homeward through the crowds to show off their buys.

As you can see, French ways are as varied as those in America or Canada, and there really is no typical French person. Rather, France is a land of many peoples, each with their own customs and traditions. Over the years, however, these peoples have developed a common way of life, characterized by a love for good food and a pride in their language.

3. The Glory of France

France's history is rich in legends of heroes and heroines, kings and queens. In days of old, singers called *troubadours* sang songs about these important men and women. Today many of these people are still celebrated in songs, stories, and festivals. They are remembered for the role they played in building the "glory of France."

Ancient France was inhabited by many tribes that spoke the Celtic language. When Julius Caesar, a Roman general, invaded the land, he found the fiercest fighters to be a tribe called the Gauls. Because of their fierceness, and the fact that Caesar probably never noticed the differences between the various Celtic tribes, he named the country Gaul after them.

A Germanic tribe called the Franks later overran the Gauls and conquered the land. Charlemagne, the Franks' greatest king, was one of the most powerful rulers who ever lived. His empire sprawled across most of western Europe.

Charlemagne was a clever and wise ruler, but he could also be very cruel. When he conquered the Saxons in Brittany, he wanted them to become Christians and be full citizens of his empire. He passed laws making it illegal not to observe Christian ways. But the Saxons were used to worshipping many gods and resisted his will. As a result, many of them were tortured and killed, and in the end Charlemagne had his way.

Despite his cruelties, Charlemagne thought it was important to educate his subjects. He started a school at his palace to train people as teachers. These people were then sent throughout the empire to give lessons in reading, writing, and arithmetic to all who wanted to learn.

Charlemagne's empire held together until his death. Then it was divided equally among his grandsons because his son had already died. Louis, his eldest grandson, received the German lands. The French-speaking countries went to Charles the Bald. And Lothair, the youngest, was given the lowlands between the other two realms. The modern states of Germany, France, and Belgium had their beginning in these divisions.

When Charles the Bald was made king in A.D. 842, France became a separate nation for the first time in its history. Yet it took another six hundred years for the French kings to become as powerful as Charlemagne had been.

One reason why the French kings were so weak is that they owned little land, which in those days was

The Glory of France

the source of wealth and power. The biggest landowners were the church and the nobles. They, not the kings, really controlled the country.

France was not an easy place to live in at this time. Roads were in very bad shape and unsafe to travel. In addition, forests were filled with robbers and cutthroats. But nobles had their own armies to protect their lands and friends.

The common people looked to the nobles or to the church for safety. Many of them worked the nobles' lands in return for their protection. In fact, the peasants depended so heavily on the nobles that they were almost like slaves. Because the nobles were so powerful, France's kings leaned heavily on them to keep the peace. But the crown's interests and those of the nobles were not always the same. As a result, they often fought each other, trying to gain more land and more power. Even the queens of France played active roles against their kings.

Eleanor of Aquitaine was one of the most powerful and strong-willed women of her time. As queen of France and later of England, she took an active interest in ruling her country.

Eleanor was the daughter of the duke of Aquitaine, an important noble. At the age of fifteen, she married King Louis VII of France. When she did, the enormous lands she had inherited, which covered nearly the western half of modern France, became part of Louis's kingdom. Eleanor never loved Louis, though, and she thought he was weak. And so when she discovered that they were too closely related for her to be his legal wife, their marriage was ended.

Shortly afterwards Eleanor married her second husband, Henry II of England. Her French lands then became English, and from Normandy to the Basque country, people began to favor English ways. So strong was England's influence that some French nobles turned against other ones. Their conflict began a one-hundred-year struggle to put an English king on the French throne.

Even Queen Isabel, wife of Charles VI of France, tried to help the English cause. She plotted with Henry V of England and the king's brothers to have the weak-minded Charles sign the Treaty of Troyes. According to the treaty's terms, Henry would marry Charles's daughter on the French king's death. In this way, Henry V would inherit the French crown.

When Isabel's plot was discovered, troubadours sang out against it. They chanted that France had been lost by a woman and could only be saved by one.

Their songs set the stage for Joan of Arc, France's greatest heroine. Though Joan was a simple shepherd-

Many artists have done paintings or made sculptures of Joan of Arc, France's greatest heroine.

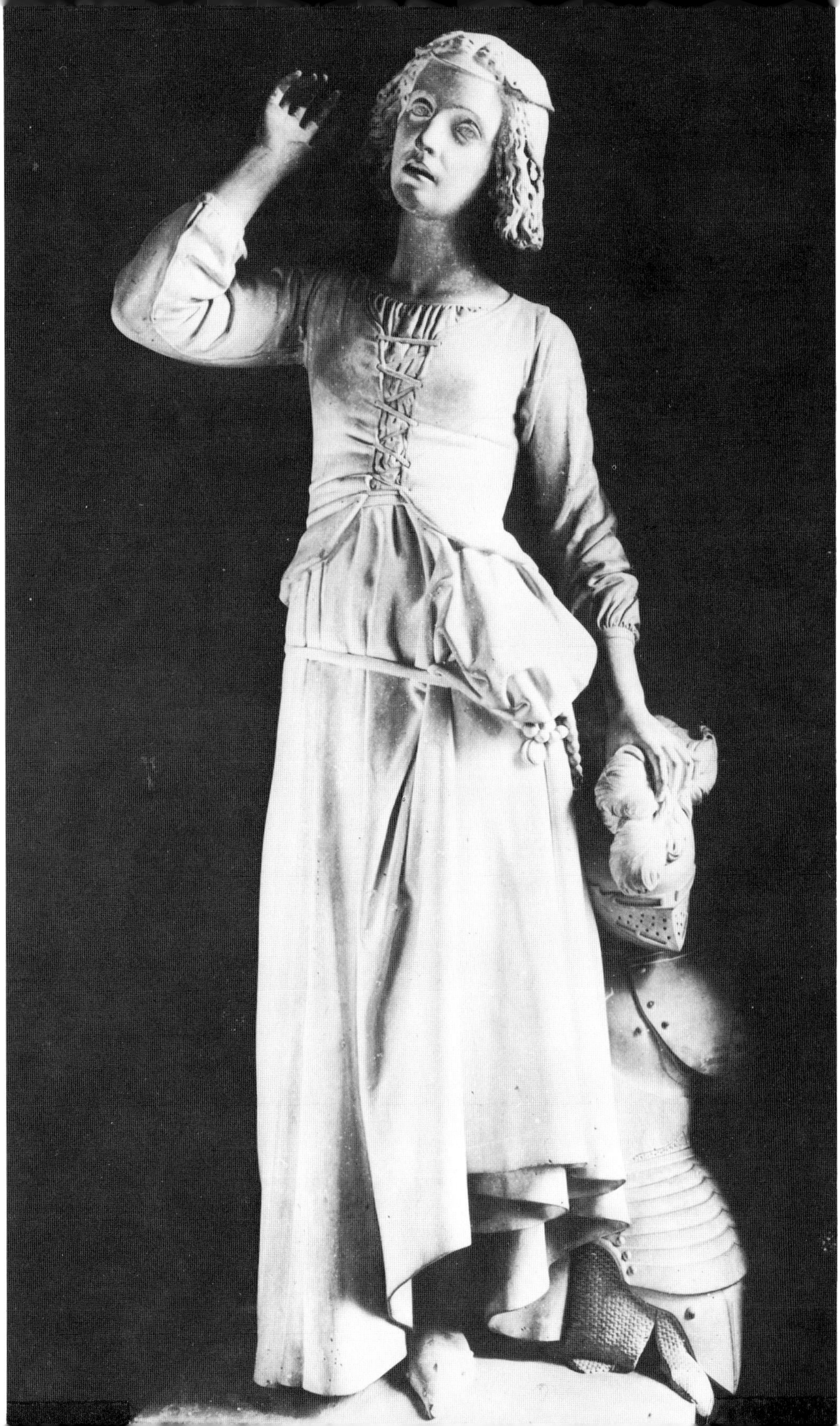

ess from the northern village of Domrémy, she became the symbol of French victory over the English. Her dreams and visions gave the people new faith.

Joan said that she was inspired to fight for France by the "voices" of the saints she heard. When she was first brought to the young uncrowned French king, Charles VII, he was unsure he could believe in her. Legends say that when they met at Chinon, Charles hid amidst the nobles of his court. Without hesitating, Joan walked directly over to Charles and asked his permission to go to war against the English.

Slowly but surely Joan began to win over Charles and the leaders of the church. They were impressed by her sincerity during the three weeks they spent questioning her at Poitiers. She told them the divine voices said that the siege of Orléans would be the deciding battle in ending the Hundred Years' War.

Joan was given royal troops and led them to Orléans, a city besieged for over nine months. After ten days' time, the French troops marched victoriously past the city gates with young Joan at their head. When the French recaptured Orléans, they regained their confidence and spirit. By the time Charles was officially crowned king of the French at Reims, the people were well on their way to ending English rule in their land.

Charles VII was crowned king of France at beautiful Reims Cathedral on July 16, 1429.

But Joan's life ended very sadly. During the siege of Paris, she was captured by the duke of Burgundy, who handed her over to the English. The English were desperate to break the new spirit Joan had brought to the French people. When she would not deny having heard the saints' voices, they burnt her as a witch.

Despite Joan's fight to rid France of the English, French kings remained weak until Louis XI's time. Louis was an unkind and cruel man who put a great many innocent people into prison. But for all his cruelties, Louis made France into a modern nation. He taxed his people heavily to raise a royal army. The nobles then knew that the king no longer had to rely on them to keep the peace or to defend the country.

Louis perfected the ways his government worked so that it ran smoothly. Because he was so unpopular, he had to know at all times what the nobles thought. For that reason, he began the royal postal network. This network helped Louis's spies to inform him of everything that happened anywhere in France. Louis's greatest rival, the duke of Burgundy, nicknamed him "the spider." For like a spider, Louis spun a web to trap the "flies" buzzing around his throne.

King Henry IV, who succeeded Louis, is best remembered for his kindness. Henry was a very wise king who preferred words to wars. For over thirty years French Catholics had been fighting to stop the

Henry IV brought an end to over thirty years of fighting between France's Catholics and Protestants.

spread of the new Protestant religion. Henry was a Protestant, or Huguenot, but to please his people, most of whom were Catholic, he became a Catholic himself.

Still, Henry did not forget the Huguenots who had fought so long to keep their faith. In a treaty called the Edict of Nantes, he gave them the right to worship freely. The edict also allowed the Huguenots to have armed fortresses at La Rochelle and Montpellier, two of the largest Huguenot cities. This made the Huguenots strong enough to defend themselves against possible attacks.

Henry worried a great deal about the common people and how they could make ends meet. His fondest dream was that one day all peasants could have a "chicken-in-the-pot" for their Sunday dinner.

Henry's son, Louis XIII, did not have his father's wisdom. But he did have a brilliant prime minister, Armand Jean du Plessis, Cardinal Richelieu. Richelieu's grand plan was to make the king's power the strongest in France. Louis apparently hated Richelieu, but he decided not to get rid of him. He doubtlessly knew that the cardinal would make him mighty.

Richelieu was good for the king but bad for France. He wasn't a cruel man, but he did not care if he caused pain. He took away Huguenot rights by ordering the forts that Henry IV had given them torn

Cardinal Richelieu took measures to make the king the most powerful man in France.

down. Richelieu did not want to take freedom of worship away from the Huguenots, but he did want to make sure that they would not be a threat to the king's power.

The cardinal didn't have many good ideas about money matters either. One day he'd announce that he had to raise taxes to help pay for his wars. But the next day he'd sign papers with trading companies that gave away huge royal fortunes in land, timber, and minerals in the New World.

Still, Richelieu paved the way for the golden age of French kings and Louis XIV. Louis XIV was

Louis XIV, "the Sun King," declared that he ruled by divine right, not by the consent of his subjects.

The Glory of France

also called *le roi soleil,* or "the sun king." Louis said France was his land to rule by divine right. He meant that his right to rule came directly from God, rather than from the consent of his subjects.

Louis XIV declared that France could have only one king, one law, and one faith. In 1685 he tore up the Edict of Nantes, the treaty that had preserved the Huguenot's religious freedom for nearly a hundred years. Many Huguenots feared renewed attacks against them by Catholics and fled to America or England.

Louis XIV was the last great king of France. The rulers who followed him could not command the people's respect or obedience. Louis XVI, one of his descendants, was well meaning, but not very smart. This Louis's wife, Marie Antoinette, was from Austria and a member of the Lutheran Church. Because of her faith and the fact that France and Austria had often fought each other, most French people saw her as their natural enemy.

Life was very bad for most people in France under Louis XVI. The country's peasants were very heavily taxed. In addition, they were tied to the land in much the same way that they had been for nearly a thousand years. The peasants worked the nobles' lands for next to nothing in return for their protection.

The middle class was made up of bankers, shopkeepers, and craftspersons. Most of them could read and write fairly well, and they worked hard for their money. A tremendous amount of what they earned had to be paid out in taxes, however.

The nobles, on the other hand, were not taxed, since their money and lands were inherited and not earned. They were also allowed more freedom than the peasants or the middle class. In fact, the laws that applied to the nobles were entirely separate from the laws that ordinary people had to obey.

The middle and peasant classes needed each other to win more freedom. Eventually, they banded together to fight against the privileges enjoyed by the king and the nobles. Representatives of the two classes withdrew from the States-General, the country's national assembly, and formed their own lawmaking body. Louis XVI ordered this group to disband, but its members refused. Inspired by their refusal, the people of Paris stormed La Bastille, a fortress where many political prisoners were kept, on July 14, 1789. Though there were only about a dozen prisoners in the Bastille at the time, this action sparked a revolution against the upper class. The storming of the fortress was such an important event that Bastille Day is now celebrated as France's Independence Day.

The storming of the Bastille on July 14, 1789 began a widespread revolt that led to major changes in French life.

By August 1789 the new lawmaking body had drawn up a Declaration of the Rights of Man and the Citizen. For the first time, freedom was set forth as a right belonging to every citizen. A good deal more fighting took place before the nobles and the king agreed that all people should be equal, though. Many members of the upper class, including Louis XVI and Marie Antoinette, were beheaded by the revolutionaries. This bloody Reign of Terror came to an end when the new leaders began to disagree and struggled for power among themselves. Afterwards, the middle

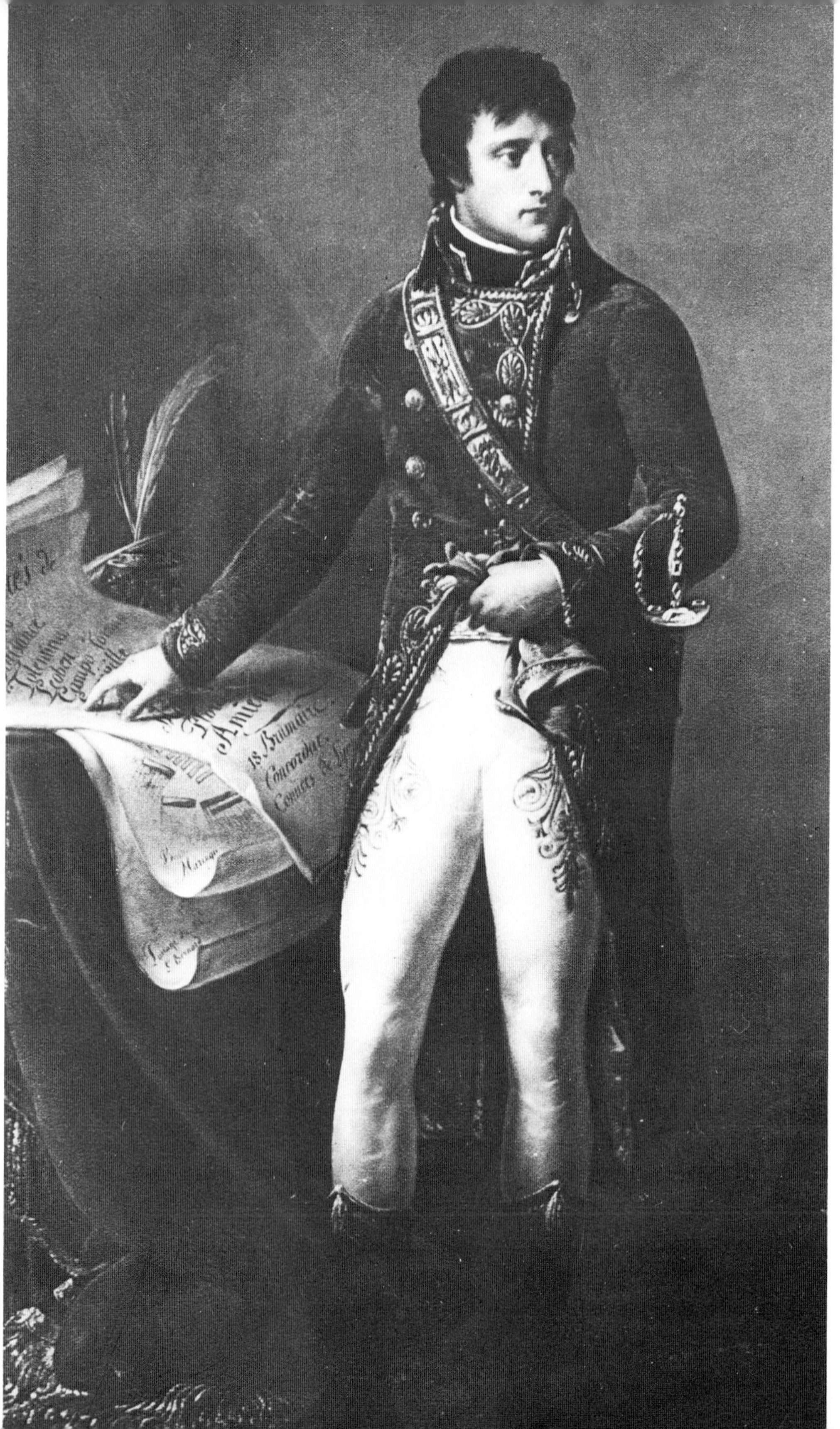
18. Brumaire
Concordat

The Glory of France

class and the peasants set about making a more democratic government.

Among the many important figures who played a role in the French Revolution was Napoleon Bonaparte. At the start of the revolt he was an artillery officer in the French army. Later he joined the revolutionary cause and led troops against the king's forces. Because of his skill and success, he was eventually made a commander in the new government's army.

In 1799 Bonaparte was in Egypt, waging war against Turkey and Great Britain. Word came to him that the French government was losing its power. Turning over command of his army to another general, he made his way back to Paris. There, on November 9, 1799, he and his followers seized control of the country.

The man his troops called "puss-in-boots" soon became France's new ruler. At first he was titled First Consul in the new three-member government known as the Consulate. But he was not satisfied with his position, and he gradually began to take complete control of the government. He achieved this goal in 1804, when the French senate made him emperor.

Napoleon dreamed of making France as large and powerful as it had been in Charlemagne's time.

Bonaparte became the First Consul of France in 1799. Five years later he was made Emperor Napoleon I.

Through the various wars that he fought he became King of Italy and Protector of the Rhine Confederation, the lands on the west bank of the Rhine River. But this wasn't enough for Napoleon, and he fought other wars to try to expand his empire. Sending his troops into Austria, Prussia, and Russia, he managed to conquer most of Europe by 1812.

Though many French people link Napoleon's name with wars, he was responsible for many other great triumphs. For example, when he invaded Russia, he saw that his food supplies would grow scarce because of that country's cold, snowy winters. After a long search, Napoleon finally found a candymaker named Nicolas Appert to help solve this problem. Appert sealed all kinds of cooked food inside champagne bottles. Then he heated them in boiling water for varying lengths of time, depending on what the bottles contained. This method, which kept the food from spoiling, helped Napoleon provide for his troops. It also made Appert somewhat famous. Today he is credited with having developed the very first canning process.

Napoleon was also a remarkable organizer. He saw that the divisions of the different regions in France no longer matched the needs of the people. To deal with this situation he created the *départements* or administrative districts, of modern day France, each governed by a prefect. These départements are currently administered by a locally elected council. The prefect is now called a commissioner.

Bonaparte's highest achievement was his Code Napoléon, a set of strict laws for society. The code gave every person in France the right to own property. It also stated that the laws would apply to everyone in the same way.

The Code Napoléon was so good that it is still the law in France today. But did you know that many laws from the code are also observed in Louisiana? These laws have been in effect since 1803, when President Thomas Jefferson bought the Louisiana Territory from Napoleon.

Despite his many accomplishments, Napoleon could not conquer his own pride and ambition. He eventually took on too many European enemies at one time and was finally defeated at Waterloo, a Belgian town, in 1815. Later he was exiled to the island of Saint Helena, off the southwest coast of Africa, where he died in 1821.

The former French nobles saw the defeat of Napoleon as their chance to bring back the king and their old ways. In 1814 they put Louis XVIII on the throne. But after sixteen years the people revolted, and the second French republic was formed, with Louis Napoleon Bonaparte, a nephew of Napoleon, as its president. Louis was not satisfied just to be president, however. He gradually took on more and more power and finally declared himself Emperor Napoleon III in 1852.

France flourished under Louis Napoleon's government. The Industrial Revolution was just beginning, and the atmosphere for growth was perfect. Many job and investment opportunities opened up across the land. Bridges, railways, docks, and even sewer systems were built throughout Europe using French engineers and money. Many Jewish and Protestant businessmen were encouraged to set up trade, and they greatly contributed to France's wealth.

The French became concerned about the rising power of Germany during Louis Napoleon's reign. Patriots convinced the emperor that he should go to war against the German states, which were being led by Prussia's Otto von Bismarck. Germany defeated France in this war, forcing Louis Napoleon to resign. It also took the French lands of Alsace and Lorraine, which remained part of Germany until after World War I.

Wars have always changed France enormously. World War II saw two French governments ruling at the same time. The southern part of France was governed at Vichy by Marshal Henri Philippe Pétain. The northern two-thirds of the country were controlled by the Germans. Because Pétain largely co-

The Glory of France

operated with the Germans, all of France was really under their power. General Charles de Gaulle would not accept the German rule. Fleeing to London, he urged French citizens to join the Free France movement and resist the Germans. Because he left France carrying only a small suitcase, some people said that he held the honor of the country in his hand.

After the war, de Gaulle tried to build a new France. Because there were many political parties, he wanted to have a strong president and a weak national assembly. In this way, the president could rise above party differences and guide the land with a firm hand. When the people voted against this idea, de Gaulle resigned.

In 1958 France's leaders realized that de Gaulle was right. He was asked to return from retirement and draft a new constitution for the nation.

De Gaulle was a man of vision, and like many leaders before him, he believed in the "glory of France." De Gaulle dreamed of a strong Western Europe, with its various countries related to one another like states within the same union. To bring these nations together, he supported the European Community, or European Common Market, a trade organization. He also tried to keep France and Western Europe free of foreign influence, especially from the United States and the Soviet Union.

In April 1969 de Gaulle resigned from office because voters would not approve some constitutional reforms he supported. He was succeeded by Georges Pompidou, who continued some of his policies but changed others. In particular, Pompidou worked to improve relations with Great Britain and the United States.

Pompidou died in April 1974. Afterwards, the Gaullist Party, which had supported him, lost its power. When elections were held in May 1974, Valéry Giscard d'Estaing, head of the Independent Republican Party, was chosen president. To maintain his power, d'Estaing had to please many different groups. His policies did not prove to be popular with most French people, however. In 1981 he was voted out of office in favor of François Mitterand, the Socialist Party candidate.

Now a new chapter in French history has begun. Under Mitterand the government has taken over more control of French businesses. It has also given locally elected councils responsibility for administering France's départements. These changes, as well as some of Mitterand's other policies, have made some French people unhappy. That is why only time will tell if he, too, shall become a hero in the spirit of the "glory of France."

4. Of Little People and Tall Tales

If you're out on a lonely field in France, be ready for the unexpected. The land is just bubbling with all sorts of little people, elves, and goblins. In Lorraine, water fairies called *ondines* nibble at toes dangling over the sides of boats. High in the Alps, *solèves* work their elfin magic. They'll help you in your garden just when all looks hopeless. And in Normandy, goblins wash your windows and care for your livestock. You must be kind to them in return, though, or else they'll do a lot of mischief.

Tales, superstitions, and legends about imaginary folk are very important in France. They give expression to people's feelings and beliefs. In addition, they are a form of entertainment that everyone can enjoy.

Many French folktales have their roots in history. The people of Provence, for example, tell stories about the Moors, Arabs from northern Africa who conquered almost all of Spain and southern France before Charlemagne's time. These Moors ruled Provence for over two hundred years. During that time, the people there told stories about vast fortunes in gold and silver that the Arab invaders had supposedly buried throughout the countryside. These treasures were said to be watched over by *la chèvre d'or,* or "the golden-fleeced goat."

According to one tale, a Moorish ruler, or *émir*, stashed his treasure in caves on the mountains of Cordes, near Arles. A golden-horned goat was said to guard the sword-shaped entrance to these caves. Many people have reported seeing this creature over the centuries, but the entrance to the caves has never been found.

Another Provençal folktale says that a peasant named Janet stumbled across the golden goat's lands at Tanneron in the département of Le Var. Janet was chasing a wild boar when he heard strange noises in a thicket. When he came nearer, Janet saw a splendid golden-fleeced goat whose golden horns had become tangled in the brambles. The peasant cut the animal loose with his knife and freed him. Much to Janet's surprise, the goat said, "Follow me."

He was shown the caves where the golden goat guarded untold fortunes in gold and silver. Then thanking Janet for his kindness, the animal told him to take as much of the treasure as he could carry away.

Janet obeyed and left Tanneron with his fortune. He traveled around the world and saw and learned many things he never knew existed. Yet no matter where he went or what he did, Janet could find no happiness. When he returned home, he kept repeating the story of his meeting with la chèvre d'or to the young, hoping they could learn from his mistakes. Janet had discovered that it is better to have a simple and peaceful life than one of false joys bought by wealth too easily earned.

The city of Marseille is the capital of the département of Provence Côte d'Azur. It is also a place where fact and fiction become interwoven. The people of the city, the *Marseillais*, are known throughout France as tellers of tall tales *par excellence.* In fact, when the French remark, "Oh, you must be from Marseille," they are nicely saying that they think a person is exaggerating, or stretching the truth.

One of their folktales shows that the Marseillais are aware that they do sometimes exaggerate. This story, which deals with *le gros poisson*, or "the great fish," tells of the adventures of an apprentice named Genèsi, who lived in the suburb of Martigues. Each day he went into Marseille on business, not returning to his village until late at night. At each homecoming, Genèsi's friends crowded around him, asking him question after question about life in the big city. After months of trying to answer everyone, the weary Genèsi decided to tell his friends the biggest lie he could imagine in order to keep them quiet.

The next time he returned from Marseille, Genèsi was ready. "This morning," he announced to all, "an enormous fish swam into the harbor at Marseille. It was not merely a large fish, mind you. This fish had its head pressed tightly against the harbor walls. Its tail lay across the bay, all the way to the island of the Château d'If, where Monsieur Dumas said the Count of Monte Cristo was imprisoned."

All who heard the tale thought this great fish was surely worth seeing. When Genèsi saw them leaving for Marseille, he couldn't help but laugh. But after a time he began to wonder. If the villagers were going to town to see this fish of his, perhaps he should go, too. After all, the story he had told just might be true.

The people of Marseille are not the only ones who tell these kinds of stories. In fact, folktales from other parts of France can be just as full of exaggeration. A good example is the Gascon folk legend about the mysterious *drac*.

Dracs are supposed to be tiny spirits who like horses and stables. During the day, they hide in the horses' trough, or even in cracks in the barn walls. As soon as the moon rises, they spring from their secret homes.

Dracs live in this way because they don't like the sight of people. As a matter of fact, if a person meddles with dracs, any kind of mischief can happen.

But not all people are unhappy to have these creatures living in their stables. Long after they have gone to bed, the dracs can be heard whistling while grooming the horses. Some farmers claim that the dracs care for horses better than most stable helpers.

Still, having dracs does have its drawbacks. If a farmer locks up the oats bin overnight, the dracs are likely to break into it and eat up all the grain. You see, oats are their favorite dinner, and they get very angry when they think that the farmer doesn't trust them.

Most French farmers agree that dracs should be avoided. Should you come across one in or around a stable, they say, pretend the creature isn't there. Otherwise, you might find yourself covered with mud or soaked through with the horses' water.

Troublesome as dracs can be, they are not nearly as mischievous as the *koligans* of Brittany. These dwarves live in and around the ancient druid temples at Carnac. The temples' large upright stones, or menhirs, are perfect cover for koligans on the prowl for unsuspecting victims. They can easily sneak up behind you and drag you off by the hair, to do with you as they please.

Many Bretons say they've heard and seen koligans singing and dancing on the moors in the evening mists. You may not believe them. But do be careful if you stroll near Carnac at night. The shadows dancing about in the fog just may not be twisted trees or even menhirs.

The huge menhirs at Carnac provide a perfect hiding place for mischievous koligans.

Unlike the koligans of Brittany, *les petits hommes cornus*, or "little horned men," of Lorraine do not make trouble for people. They often help little boys and girls who have lost their way in the forest. They are also the keepers of a tremendous fortune in gold. But unless the gold is kept underground, it will turn red, making it useless to them.

How can you tell these little men from koligans? Well, for one thing les petits hommes cornus have a horn right in the middle of their forehead. Secondly, they are barely one foot tall and live underground or in the cracks of mountains. Thirdly, like gnomes, they have long white hair and beards. Finally, the horned men always wear red and carry silver spears.

Just about the only thing that people do to anger these tiny fellows is to scream like geese. The horned men are afraid of these great birds because they chase them and peck at them with their beaks.

The mysteries of France are not limited to its little folk. You may remember that Brittany, Normandy, and Aquitaine were also part of England at one time. For ten years they were ruled by England's King Richard I, or Richard the Lion-Hearted. Near the end of his reign, Richard left England to put down a revolt in Normandy. Instead, he met a mysterious death in Haute-Vienne, part of his Aquitaine inheritance.

According to legend, Richard laid siege to the Château of Châlus to dig up buried treasure belonging to the duke of Limoges. While digging, he was caught in a surprise attack and killed.

In 1963, in the shadow of the château where Richard I died, a peasant named Ramand was clearing his field. Ramand stopped work to dig out what he thought were boulders. Instead, he had unearthed 115 ancient gold pieces worth over 300,000 French francs, or about $60,000. Was this actually the same fortune Richard had been looking for almost seven hundred years earlier? No one can say for sure.

Besides their tales and legends, the French have many old sayings that express their feelings and beliefs. Sometimes these sayings deal with things or events that are supposed to bring good or bad luck. How many times have you heard, "Step on a crack, break your mother's back"? French children don't have this saying, but their language is rich with many others. One of them is a rhyme that goes:

> The first one to see:
> Spiders in the morning, mean bad luck's warning;
> Spiders in the afternoon, mean you'll receive presents soon;
> Spiders in the evening, will see new hope ripening.

Of Little People and Tall Tales

In some French homes you'll never find a loaf of bread turned on its side or upside down. According to an old saying, that would bring bad luck. Some French people won't give household knives or scissors as presents either. They've heard a saying that such gifts may "cut" their friendship with the person to whom they were given.

A great number of old sayings have been influenced by tales of little people dancing under moonlit skies. According to some of these sayings, each of the moon's various "faces" foretells a certain kind of adventure. Others say that if you cut your hair at the time of the new moon, it will grow back faster—but it may also fall out while you are still young!

The French have also said that children born at the time of the new moon will talk constantly, while those born on a moonless night will be very intelligent. Even laziness has been connected to the moon in a saying. Before you start your work, it advises, ask the moon its age. Then wait for its answer before you begin!

These French folktales, legends, and sayings are as much a part of France as its land, history, and language. They knit together past with present, fact with fiction. And in so doing they give France a special warmth and charm.

5. Days to Make Merry

Let's say it's November 25, and you're in Paris. While walking through the streets, you look up and see a group of young women coming toward you. Their dresses are modern, but they're wearing old-fashioned bonnets made of paper, lace, and ribbons. Now wouldn't you ask yourself, Why are they dressed that way? Well, it may be Thanksgiving time in America, but in France it's Saint Catherine's Day. And on this day unmarried French women twenty-five years or older put on handmade hats.

Perhaps you thought that French holidays and festivals were much the same as American ones. Now it is true that New Year's Day, Easter, and Christmas are celebrated in France. But what of Columbus Day or Thanksgiving? On these American holidays, life in France goes on as usual, and most French people don't even know they exist. The French Feast of the Kings and Old Maid's Day are equally hard for most Americans to imagine. Yet in spite of our differences, you would be surprised at how much the French have contributed to some of our merrymaking.

In France, as in Canada and America, people begin celebrating the new year on December 31 with a feast called a *réveillon*. When the old year ends, everyone cries, *bonne année*, "Happy New Year." New Year's Day is a time for good friends to go out together and have fun. Many people exchange special gifts called *les étrennes*, or "the brand news." (When you put something on or use it for the very first time, it is called an *étrenne*.) These gifts are said to bring good luck.

January 6, Epiphany, was originally a religious holiday. It honored the three Wise Men who brought gifts to the Christ child. Long ago it was also called Twelfth Night because it was celebrated on the twelfth night after Christmas.

Today Epiphany is entirely reserved for children. They gather happily each year to *tirer le roi*, or "draw out the king." To do this, a large, round, puffy pastry called *la galette des rois* is baked with a single bean inside it. This bean represents the king. The youngest child in the group cuts la galette and gives out the pieces to his friends at random. The child who finds the bean—hopefully before it is eaten—becomes the king or queen for the festivities. Then he or she chooses a royal mate. The royal couple is given a gold and silver paper crown, while their friends drink and eat to their health.

February 2 is Groundhog Day in America, but in France it is *la Chandeleur*, or Candlemas. This was

Children hope to find the lucky bean in the galette des rois, a pastry baked on Epiphany.

first a Catholic holy day, remembered by a mass, or church service, in which candles were blessed and carried in a procession. Today Candlemas has become a family holiday as well.

Young and old enjoy the *crêpe* flipping at Candlemas regardless of their religion. Crêpes are thin, liquidy pancakes which are quickly pan fried on both sides. Jams and jellies, or vegetables and meats in cream sauces are spread on the open crêpe. Then the crêpe is rolled up and eaten while it is still warm. The Candlemas legend encourages everyone in the family to try his or her luck at flipping crêpes. It says that if you flip your crêpes while holding a coin, you will have happiness and wealth in the coming year.

Like Candlemas, Shrove Tuesday is both a religious and family holiday. Long ago this feast, now called Mardi Gras in both French and English, was made by and for children. Young people had their own roosters, and they brought them to school for cockfights. They played all sorts of ball games while their parents watched the festivities. No one above school age was allowed to join in the fun. In the evening, the children would dress up in masked costumes and dance in the streets.

Today adults join in the gaiety, too. Since Mardi Gras is also the last day before Lent begins, there are hearty feasts everywhere. Children and their parents assemble giant flowered floats for the boulevard parades.

Did you know that we owe one of our funniest days to the French? *Poisson d'avril*, or April Fools' Day, came about because of a French king. April 1 used to be New Year's Day. But towards the end of the 1500s, Charles IX changed it. From then on, January 1 was the beginning of the year. People felt they just couldn't let April 1 go by like any other day, though, and so they began to play tricks on one another.

Nowadays, it is chiefly children who pull the pranks. The most common trick is to try to hang a paper fish on the back of an adult without being caught. If the children succeed, the adult is supposed to treat them to a chocolate fish.

French children celebrate Easter in much the same way that we do. It is a combination of church-going, Sunday finery, and Easter egg hunts. But there is an Eastertime legend which is wholly French. In France, the church bells are silent from Good Friday to Easter Sunday. The legend says that the bells have left the country for a trip to Rome during this time and that they will return on Easter Sunday, weighted down with gifts for the children.

We also have the French to thank for one of our most loved holiday decoratons. A *sapin de Noël*, or

A delicious bûche de Noël cake is served for dessert at the feast held on Christmas Eve.

"Christmas tree," glittered for the first time on this day in Alsace in 1605. The Alsacians say it reminds people everywhere of the beauty of the Garden of Eden. By the mid-1800s the custom of putting up a Christmas tree had spread through much of Europe and North America.

As on New Year's Eve, there is a large feast called a réveillon on Christmas Eve. The traditional dessert at this meal is a *bûche de Noël*, or "Yule log pastry." A sweet, long cake, the bûche de Noël was made to resemble the customary Yule log. Before central heating, this log was usually placed on the fire to warm the house and the Christmas dinner while families were at Midnight Mass.

Le père Noël, or Santa Claus, squeezes down chimneys in France, too. But most of the time, he does not place his gifts under the tree as he does in North America. Before going to bed on Christmas Eve, the children place their shoes beside the fireplace. When they awake on Christmas Day, they discover that Santa has stuffed the toys in or under their shoes.

We have all heard that Santa does not give presents to bad boys and girls. In France these children are punished by *le père fouettard*, or the Whip Father, who leaves them a whip instead of toys. That way there is never any doubt as to which children have been good and which have been bad.

Each French region has very different ways of celebrating Christmas. Provence is known for its lively songfests before Midnight Mass. The children there create small clay figures called *santons*, or "little saints," to place into the mangers they've made at church or home. In a breathtaking scene, the children and adults of the département of La Savoie ski down the slopes of the Alps at night by torchlight. And the winegrowers of Briançon in Burgundy come to church yearly without fail to hear the special ceremony blessing the year's best wines.

Days to Make Merry

There are many festive occasions in France which are not strictly religious ones. One of the most colorful of these in rural France is Saint John's Day. This holiday, which dates back over fifteen hundred years, takes place on June 24. Huge blazes of wood and hay are lit to honor the beginning of summer. Since the time of the Middle Ages, the fires have also marked the birthday of Saint John the Baptist. He is remembered as the prophet who baptized Jesus Christ and prepared the way for his ministry.

Les feux de la Saint Jean, or "Saint John's fires," light up the night in the French countryside. As in olden times, young couples will sometimes jump over the fires. Children and their parents dance around them singing old folk tunes. Often, people named *Jean* or *Jeanne* will wake the next morning to find their homes beautifully trimmed with flowers and greenery.

French children do not go trick-or-treating because their country no longer celebrates Halloween. Still, some of our Halloween ways come from France. You'll remember that the Gauls were one of many Celtic tribes in ancient France. These Celts believed that the souls of the dead returned to their homes on a certain evening in the fall. That's why we imagine that ghosts, witches, hobgoblins, and demons of all sorts roam about on the night of October 31.

Our ways of dressing up and our parties come from a separate French children's holiday called *la masquérade du Cherubim*. On November 4, all the children would disguise themselves in fanciful costumes and go out dancing. Over the years, this children's holiday has completely vanished because of the solemn religious celebration of All Saints' Day that occurs on November 1.

We couldn't take a look at merrymaking in France without mentioning feasts. In chapter two you learned that each wine region has its own special festival to celebrate the grape harvest. But just think, the oldest food festival in France dates back to the year 1222! Known as *La foire au Jambon*, or Ham Feast, it takes place from the evening of Palm Sunday to Easter Day on the Boulevard Richard Lenoir in Paris. Young and old alike flock there to taste thousands of mouth-watering ham dishes.

The ham has its very own festival at this time for two reasons. First, it is a French way to end the season of Lent by eating a specially cooked ham. Second, pigs were the first goods traded in peace between the Gauls and the Romans, and the French want to honor the animals for their role in history.

You have had a glimpse of what French holidays mean. They are a time for remembering important people and events from the past. In addition, they are

Days to Make Merry

times when family members can enjoy one another's company. Everyday worries about work and school seem to vanish when people gather together to make merry. Holidays, then, not only serve to help the French observe special occasions, but they also help to strengthen family ties.

6. At Home and in the Kitchen

Every French city, town, and village has a mixture of old and new buildings. In the cities, where most people live, you will find some families living in houses that are over two hundred years old. Known as *hôtels particuliers*, these large private houses stand behind sturdy *portes cochères* ("courtyard doors") that border the sidewalks. Many of these hôtels have been divided into smaller apartments because they cost too much for one family to own. Other families live in modern apartment buildings or in smaller private homes called *villas*.

The French have used a variety of materials to build their homes. Quite a few mountain towns and villages have wooden *chalets* ("cottages") nestled in the hillsides. City homes are usually made of cement blocks, steel, stone, and plaster. Many of the country's great historic *châteaux* ("castles") are built of very large stones.

No matter what French houses are made of or where they are located, they have certain features in common. Most have large picture windows which open outwards. Since these windows must be pushed open, people generally don't put screens on them.

At Home and in the Kitchen

Most French homes also have large, spacious kitchens. Cooking and good food are very important in France, and so builders are careful to make kitchens both practical and roomy.

Depending on people's tastes, French homes may have modern, antique, or country furniture. Antique pieces are usually over a hundred years old. Some people have chairs, tables, or beds that were popular with four French kings named Louis. These kings, numbered XIII, XIV, XV, and XVI, each preferred a particular style of furniture. Today we can tell which pieces were made during each king's rule. Rustic, or country, furniture is usually very simple, yet elegant. Most rustic pieces are made from the trunks of very large dark oak trees. Many French people like this kind of furniture because it gives a warm feeling to a room. Still others prefer very modern styles made from such materials as glass, aluminum, plywood, and molded plastic.

Life in Paris or any of the other big French cities is very busy. As a matter of fact, it is not all that different from life in New York or Toronto. People work from early in the morning until five or six o'clock at night. At lunchtime, they usually eat a sandwich at the office cafeteria or corner *café*. Most schools have cafeterias, too, and so students don't go home for lunch either. City people also depend

This colorfully roofed old building is a hospice, a shelter for travelers.

Many French people live in very modern apartment buildings, such as this one in Paris.

heavily on the telephone. Indeed, telephones are everywhere, and they are used constantly.

But what about the smaller cities, towns, and farm villages? About one-quarter of all French people still make their homes in these areas. In some ways, their lives are more relaxed than those of city people. Entire towns close up between noon and two o'clock so that everyone can go home for lunch. Telephones are thought to be an unnecessary expense. Most people still shop at small neighborhood stores for most of their needs. Many times a shopkeeper will sell them food on credit if they're low on cash. The nicest thing of all is that almost everyone living in their part of town knows them by sight.

Farm children have a somewhat harder life than city children. Most are expected to do their chores before going to school. When they come home again at night, there are evening chores to do as well.

No matter where or how people live in France, their daily lives center on their families. Because of this, French children are very well cared for. Indeed, it is safe to say that most of a family's energy is spent in helping each child grow into a happy, responsible person. Even the government has helped by making laws to protect children's rights. Government officials carefully examine everything from school programs to TV commercials. If they find things that might be harmful to children, a program or product must be changed.

Although French families differ in many ways, they have certain characteristics in common. For one thing, in more and more families both parents must work to make ends meet. New laws have helped to make bringing up children a bit easier, though. The French social security system pays most of a family's medical bills. Other medical expenses are covered by low cost group health insurance policies.

Both parents are allowed a leave from work when their baby is born. This leave can last for quite a long time. Let's say a father wishes to raise the new baby. He would be permitted to be away from his job for up to two years. At the end of that time, the law says his boss must give him his old job back. If his old job is taken, he must be offered one almost like it.

Many people feel that it has become too expensive to raise a large family. For this reason, France's population has been growing very slowly. Since 1945 it has increased by about one percent a year. *Le complément familial,* or "family supplement," was created to change this situation. Even if the mother works, a family with three children receives extra money each month. By helping out the larger families, the government hopes to encourage couples to have more children. It believes this method is the best way

The French place a high value on family life.

At Home and in the Kitchen

to make sure that the country will have enough workers in the years to come.

Most adults are on the job from 8:00 A.M. to 6:00 P.M., with two hours off for lunch. But if you happen to own a neighborhood *boulangerie*, or "bread shop," you might have to be at work by 3:00 or 4:00 A.M. in order to start your baking.

Except in the largest cities, lunch is still the biggest meal of the day in France. Many people in small cities and towns eat it at home with their families because they live close to the place they work. It's rather nice for these families to be able to spend this time together.

The French love their children and love being around them. Still, parents expect them to be well behaved and courteous. It is rare to see a French child yell or scream in public.

French children seem to be aware that their parents work very hard, and so they usually help out around home. Some children do the grocery shopping at small neighborhood stores. Others set the table or even start dinner, especially if both parents work.

Most French children like to spend time with their grandparents. In some families, the parents, children, and grandparents live in the same house. More often, the grandparents live close by. If they do, the children and their parents usually come to their homes for Sunday dinner, the week's most enjoyable meal. Afterwards, the entire family may go to a nearby park or take a quiet drive in the country. No matter what anyone does the rest of the week, Sundays belong to the family.

French families spend their evenings in much the same way that we do. After dinner, they often sit down to watch TV. They don't have a great many programs to choose from, however. For there are only three TV channels in France, all of them owned and operated by the government. Many programs from North America are shown on French television. Some are translated into French; others have French subtitles. The French also like many of the same movies and songs that are popular with North Americans.

Occasionally, the family will invite people over for the evening. When the guests arrive, *un petit café*, "a bit of coffee," is whisked to them from the kitchen. Pastries or local sweet dishes are spread out before the visitors, who usually have trouble curbing their appetites.

Delicious foods of this sort are part of every French meal. At breakfast, or *le petit déjeuner*, people often eat tasty *croissants*, or "crescent rolls." They also enjoy slices of *la baguette*, a long loaf of sourdough bread, covered with butter and jam.

City people often have lunch at sidewalk cafés, where they talk, read, or simply watch the crowds pass by.

A good French *déjeuner*, or "lunch," will include tasty meats and vegetables, a salad, and a sweet dessert. Except in the largest cities, the lunch break lasts about two hours. Even the stores close up. Of course, not all of the time is spent eating. After the meal is finished, people can talk, read, or go for a walk. That is why so many of them find lunch a nice way to relax in the middle of the day.

Pâtisseries, or "pastries," may be eaten anytime, but they are most often enjoyed at *les quatre heures*, or "four o'clocks," the French teatime or snack time.

A hot cocoa or café au lait would be served along with these sweets. Another delicious treat French children love at les quatre heures is a chocolate bar slipped into a long slice of baguette.

The French like to have a late, light dinner. A typical meal consists of soup and cold meats, with fruit, yogurt, or cheese for dessert.

Because food is such an important part of French life, it is no wonder that almost everyone enjoys preparing even the most simple meal. Nor is it surprising that the French highly regard their best cooks. Indeed, it is a great honor to be named a *grand chef de cuisine*, or "great chef." Why even the great French writers have dabbled in the kitchen. Many of you have probably heard of Alexandre Dumas's novel, *The Three Musketeers*. Did you know that Mr. Dumas had hoped that his *Dictionnaire de la Cuisine (Cooking Dictionary)* would be hailed as his masterpiece? Little did he know that his "other books," as he called them, would survive as his best works.

Not everyone in France is a great cook. Still, almost anyone can make some of the more popular dishes. In fact, French cooking is much less difficult than most people imagine.

Here are a few recipes for you to try. They are sure to delight your family and friends. Have fun making them, and *bon appétit* ("happy eating")!

Crêpes

1 cup all-purpose flour
1/4 teaspoon baking powder
1 1/4 cups milk
1 egg
1 teaspoon margarine or butter, melted

Mix flour and baking powder in medium-sized bowl. Stir in other ingredients. Beat entire mixture by hand, or with beater, until smooth. Lightly butter medium-sized skillet. Heat skillet at moderate temperature until butter bubbles.

Pour 1/4 cup crêpe batter into skillet. Immediately turn skillet from side to side so that batter covers bottom in a thin film. Cook batter until small bubbles begin to form on top of crêpe. Run a wide spatula underneath edges of crêpe to loosen it. Flip crêpe over and cook other side until it turns a golden color. Remove crêpe from skillet. Stack cooked crêpes on plate and serve warm. Serves 6.

Serving Suggestion: Set out small custard dishes filled with jellies, jams, fresh fruit slices, whipped cream, or even leftover stews. Your guests can put one of these toppings on the crêpes and then roll them up for eating.

Croque Monsieur

1 slice bread, toasted
1 slice Swiss cheese
1 slice ham
butter or margarine

Spread butter or margarine on bread. Put on ham and cheese. Place this open-faced sandwich in oven and heat at 425° F. for about 10 minutes. Remove and serve.

Three Cheese Quiche

1 3/4 cups flour, sifted
1 stick salted butter or margarine
7 tablespoons ice water
1/4 pound small curd cottage cheese
2 tablespoons milk
6 medium-sized mushrooms, sliced (optional)
1/2 cup Swiss cheese, grated
1/4 wheel bonbel-type cheese, cubed
2 eggs, beaten

Sift flour into medium-sized bowl. Cut up butter into seven or eight pieces. Make a hollow space in center of flour and add pieces of butter. Using a pastry

At Home and in the Kitchen 91

blender or your fingers, mix butter and flour into granular dough. Make another hollow space in center of grainy dough mixture. Add 7 tablespoons of ice water. Mix until water is absorbed into dough. If dough will not hold together, add 1 or 2 more tablespoons of ice water. Form dough into ball. Cover it with a damp paper towel and refrigerate for 1 hour.

Preheat oven to 400°F. Roll out pastry dough to about 1/4-inch thickness on lightly floured surface. Line a 9 or 10-inch pie pan with dough. Lightly pierce entire bottom of this pastry shell with a fork to prevent dough from puffing up. Bake shell for 10 minutes. Remove from oven and allow to cool.

Combine cottage cheese, milk, Swiss cheese, bonbel cheese, eggs, and milk in medium-sized bowl. Pour cheese mixture into pastry shell. Put shell back in oven and bake until filling turns golden color and shell light brown—about 30 to 45 minutes. Allow quiche to cool slightly before cutting into slices.

7. School Days

During the school year, most of you are probably very happy to see Friday come. But for French children, Friday isn't a special day at all. School is held on Monday, Tuesday, Thursday, Friday, and Saturday morning. Wednesdays, Saturday afternoons, and Sundays are days off. So in France, it's Wednesdays or Saturday afternoons that bring sighs of relief to weary students.

In the past, schools were run by the church, and children only learned what it thought was useful. Priests rarely taught reading or math. It seems these skills were of little use to either the church or the people. Instead, everyone learned lessons from the Bible. And it was for this reason that those who knew the Bible were called educated.

Under Napoleon, the government took control of the country's schools of higher learning. Grade schools, however, continued to be run by private citizens or by cities, and girls still received less instruction than boys. In fact, girls weren't even allowed to attend high school until about a hundred years ago.

Today any child between the ages of six and sixteen must go to school. But since nursery schools are

Most French students receive a good, but very demanding, education.

part of the public school system, about half the children start at age two.

French schools are quite different from those in North America. Let's imagine a young sixth grader named Jean Dupont. On school days, he would be awakened by his clanging alarm clock at 7:15 A.M. Quickly turning the alarm off, he would crawl out of his warm bed, dress, and have a light breakfast. By 8:30 A.M. he would be seated at his school desk.

Jean would probably start off his day in French class. This class would be followed by a lesson concerning a foreign language such as English or Spanish. Then would come history, geography, and civics,

French children are introduced to numbers and letters in nursery school.

followed by physical education. Jean would then dash home for a two-hour lunch break with his family. Once back at school, his afternoon would be jam packed, with classes in arithmetic, science, and art or music. The day would finally end at 5:00 P.M., when Jean and his classmates were dismissed.

Public education begins in nursery schools. The teachers in these schools try to make the youngsters comfortable in their new surroundings. Besides having fun, the children are introduced to numbers and letters. If they seem interested, they may even begin learning to read and write.

French children are judged by their abilities and their willingness to learn. Nevertheless, a child's needs are always put first. Let's say a four-year-old young-

School Days

ster seems ready for the demands of first grade. This child could not move on unless his or her teacher and parents agreed that he or she did not need to attend kindergarten. The child would also have to agree with this decision.

Elementary school normally starts at age six, when students enter *onzième*, "eleventh grade." That's right, eleventh grade! In France, the grades with the highest numbers have the youngest students. A student in *huitième*, "eighth grade," is normally nine or ten years old. One in *septième*, "seventh grade," would be ten or eleven.

French schools are very difficult by North American standards. Even the youngest children have long, hard days of learning—as many as thirty hours of

Tape recorders and other audiovisual devices are used to help French students learn a foreign language.

classes a week! Students in French schools also receive a more specialized education than North American youngsters. They can choose to take more classes in subjects that interest them as early as the age of twelve or thirteen. Still, they must continue to take the basic courses in French, math, history, science, physical education, and a foreign language.

This in-depth program may also lead to early career choices. For example, a boy who is fourteen years old may already know that he wants to have special job training. If his parents and teachers agree, he would enter a program called *C.P.A.*, which stands for *Cours préparatoires a l'apprentissage* ("Preparatory Course for Apprentices"). It would help him learn a skill such as welding or bricklaying. He would spend half his school hours in classes and the rest in learning the skill.

After grade school, French youngsters are admitted to *collège*, which is about the same as junior high school. The first two years of collège are called the *cycle d'observation* ("observation cycle"). During these years, parents and teachers keep a close watch on a student's progress.

Initially, all of the students in the collège take the same classes. The number of hours they spend in each class varies from subject to subject. A typical weekly schedule includes five hours of French, three hours of

French youngsters begin to learn about computers in grade school.

math, three hours of a modern foreign language, and three hours of social studies—history, geography, economics, and civics. In addition, there are three hours of experimental sciences, two hours of art, two hours of manual and technical education, and three hours of physical education.

The last two years of collège are called the *cycle d'orientation* ("orientation cycle"). During this time, students become acquainted with a subject in which they are especially interested. They also choose courses in subjects they want to study in greater detail. These courses could be in languages—the first foreign language, a second foreign language, Latin, or Greek—or in technological studies. Whatever the students choose will add about four hours a week to their already busy school schedule. They will also have to take another hour of math each week.

At the end of collège, students receive their first diploma, the *Brevet d' Etudes des Collèges* ("Certificate of Studies"), or *B.E.C.* for short. The graduating students are usually sixteen years old and about a year ahead of North American young people in their studies.

French high schools, or *lycées*, are highly specialized. For this reason there are two kinds of them. The first, the *Lycée d'Enseignement Général et Technologique* ("General and Technological Secondary School") offers a three-year program leading to a general *baccalauréat* ("degree") or a *Brevet de Technicien* ("Technical Degree").

The baccalauréat, or *"bac"*, as French students call it, is much more than a high school diploma. A student who has earned a "bac" has completed the North American equivalent of two years of college! The reason for this is that he or she has been following a very demanding course of study since the age of fourteen.

There are eight types of "bacs" high school students may earn. These are identified by groups lettered A through H. Groups A-E are designed to give students a more general, or liberal arts, education, while those in groups F-H are intended to give them a technical one. The chart on page 99 shows how these various groups are subdivided into specific subjects.

Students do not automatically receive a baccalauréat upon completing high school. They must earn

Baccalauréat Degrees Awarded by French High Schools

General Education

A—Philosophy and Liberal Arts
  A1—Latin and Greek
  A2—Latin or Greek and a second modern language
  A3—Second modern language
  A4—Second modern language and advanced French or advanced study in first modern language
  A5—Second and third modern languages
  A6—Music and Latin or Greek or a second modern language
  A7—Plastic Arts and Latin or Greek, or a second modern language
B—Economics and Social Sciences
  B1—Latin or Greek
  B2—Second modern language
C—Mathematics and Physical Sciences
D—Mathematics and Natural Sciences
D^1—Agricultural Sciences
E—Mathematics and Technology

Technical Education

F—Industrial Techniques
  F1—Mechanical Construction
  F2—Electronics
  F3—Electrotechnology
  F4—Civil Engineering
  F5—Physics
  F6—Chemistry
  F7—Biochemistry
  $F7^1$—Biology
  F8—Medical-Social Sciences
  F9—Technical Building Equipment
  F10—Microtechnology
  F11—Music or Dance
G—Tertiary (Third) Sector
  G1—Administration
  G2—Quantitative Management Techniques
  G3—Commercial Techniques
H—Computer Science

their diploma by taking a very difficult examination, part of which is written and part spoken. Only about sixty-five percent of all students taking the test will receive one of the three passing grades: better than average, very good, and excellent.

Because the test is so difficult, students who fail it must sometimes settle for a *Certificat de Fin d' Etudes Secondaires*, or "Certificate of Completion of High School." Others want a baccalauréat so badly that they will retake the test. They may prepare for it by following a special correspondence course or even by taking their senior year in high school—called *terminal*—over again. They are willing to do these things because without a baccalauréat they cannot go on to college.

The second kind of high school, the *Lycée d' Enseignement Professionel* ("Professional Secondary School"), or *L.E.P.*, prepares students for specific jobs. It awards two kinds of diplomas. One, the *B.E.P.*, which is short for *Brevet d' Etude Professionel* ("Professional Degree"), qualifies students for just about any job in business. The other, the *C.A.P.*, which stands for *Certificat d' Aptitude Professionelle* ("Professional Aptitude Certificate"), is given to students who have developed one special skill. Students who work towards a B.E.P. diploma receive a greater general education than those striving for a C.A.P.

School Days

The French public school system is really quite good. Students must work hard to pass through it, but they receive a fine education. This is one reason why private schools are not as popular in France as they are in other countries. Another reason is that public schools and schoolbooks are free to everyone.

Most private schools are run by religious groups. These groups teach their beliefs along with other subjects. They are not free to teach whatever they please, however. According to law, they must follow the same program as is given in the public schools.

The French school system may seem very complicated. You may even wonder how the students find time for their homework, or how they have any energy left for fun on their days off. Well, don't worry. Most families don't eat dinner until 7:30 or 8:00 P.M., and so youngsters have about three hours to play after school is over. And on their days off, they enjoy themselves just as much as you do.

When you think of French students, then, remember that they are much like you. Despite their different schedules, subjects, examinations, and diplomas, they try hard to do well in school. But when the school week is over, they are glad to leave their books for a time and have fun with their friends and families.

8. The French at Play

Imagine that you're looking at some children playing in a schoolyard. In one corner, you can see them rushing and running about wildly, playing a game of tag. To your left, others are giggling around the child who is "it" in a game of blind man's buff. To your right, some girls are jumping rope. And nearest you, a small group of boys and girls is playing leap frog.

Perhaps you enjoy playing some of these games. If you do, you'd have no trouble making friends with French children. They play many of the same games you do, as well as a few you may not know.

Have you ever wondered why some games are so popular, or who invented them? Maybe, then, you'd be interested to learn that tennis was first played in France in the late twelfth century. It was invented by a few high-spirited French priests.

The priests began playing *le jeu de paume*, or "palm ball," against the courtyard walls of their church building. Over the years, it became more popular to use a racket to hit the ball. The racket was also a lot easier on the player's hands.

Throughout the Middle Ages, tennis was a favorite sport for rich and poor alike. The first tennis

Sliding boards and climbing bars are commonly found on French playgrounds.

professionals appeared in the fifteenth century. They were unlike the big money winners of today, however. Instead of competing in a tournament, they earned a living making tennis rackets and keeping up the courts.

Besides inventing tennis, the French are also largely responsible for making puppets a popular children's toy. Puppets became a big hit with the French in Paris in the 1750s. They were made to look like actors, tradesmen, and shepherds. Almost every home had at least one puppet dangling above the fireplace. One of the most popular puppet figures was the *guignol*. Today the word guignol is the name of a puppet show held especially for children.

As French children grow older, they begin to take an interest in sports. Some dream of becoming a soccer star. Others want to achieve success in rugby, cycling, pelota, or track and field. But they soon learn that years of training and practice must come first.

Training for most sports usually begins in physical education classes. These classes teach sports-minded youngsters how to keep in shape, as well as how to play various sports. The government considers the classes to be an important part of a student's education. In fact, it has recently

Puppet shows, such as the one shown here, are very popular with French children.

The French at Play

directed that they be held at least one hour per day in high school.

Most schools don't have much sports equipment, however. In addition, although there are school teams for almost every sport, they compete against other teams less often than is the case in Canada or the United States. Games are usually played in small stadiums, and there are no marching bands or cheerleaders.

Because of this situation, school coaches will often tell their best students to go to private clubs. These clubs not only have special equipment, but they also frequently compete with each other. Students who belong to them may travel anywhere in France to play in a meet.

Soccer, or *le football*, is to the French what baseball is to Americans. Adults and children glue themselves to their TV sets whenever their favorite team plays. Thousands flock to the stadiums to cheer on *les footballeurs*, or "soccer players." It is not unusual for France's largest stadium, Le Parc des Princes in Paris, to be sold out weeks before a game.

There are scores of amateur soccer teams throughout France. Even the littlest farm village is sure to have its regular soccer matches. The country also has over thirty professional soccer teams. The best players from these teams are chosen to be on L'Equipe de

France, or "The French National Team." This team plays in international matches against other countries. These matches are almost always exciting ones to watch.

France's old ties to England are clear from the people's love for rugby. There is even a special match between France, England, Ireland, Scotland, and Wales each year. It is called the Tournament of Five Nations.

Rugby is played with an oval ball that looks something like an American football. There can be either thirteen or fifteen players on a team, and the game's rules change according to their number. The object of it is always the same, though—to score points by kicking the ball over the opponent's goal or by touching it down behind the goal line. The team that scores the most points wins the game.

Though rugby resembles American football, it is still quite different. Play is much less formal, and there are few or no time-outs. No forward passes are allowed, but the ball may be thrown sideways. It is also illegal to run interference for the ball carrier. This may be one reason why the carrier often ends up being buried beneath a tackle made by half of the opposing team!

In contrast to rugby, pelota is a truly French game. *La pelote basque*, or "Basque pelota," was first

These schoolboys are playing rugby, one of France's most popular sports.

played in the Basque country of southwest France. Pelota is also the forerunner of jai alai and handball.

A favorite Parisian pastime is to go watch a pelota match at the Fronton de Paris on Sundays. The game is played on a concrete court, at one end of which is a large wall called *le fronton*. Only two people play at one time. The ball, *la pelote*, is palm-sized, has a rubber core, and is covered with a dried goatskin.

The game is played by smacking this ball against the wall with a wicker racket or with your bare hand. Then the opposing player must hit it back against the wall. The ball cannot bounce more than once. If it does, the point goes to the other player.

One of the biggest French sports events is a bicycle race that takes place each summer. Known as the Tour de France, it has everyone buzzing with excitement for the few weeks that it lasts. Thousands of people line the 2,500-mile (4,000-kilometer) course to cheer on their favorites. The cyclists have to be extremely fit to race in *le tour*. They travel on regular roads and highways throughout the land. Some of the steepest mountain passes in the world are part of the course.

The T-shirts worn by the racers have different meanings. A polka-dotted T-shirt will be worn by the best mountain sprinter, while the most competitive cyclist is given a green T-shirt. The man wearing the *maillot jaune*, or "yellow T-shirt," each day has the best time for that part of the race which has been completed. All the cyclists in the race can easily spot this person, and they all try to win the shirt away from him.

Amateur cycling is also very popular with the French. They have always been among the best cyclists in the world. As a matter of fact, the French were world champions in cycling for over ten years not too long ago.

You may think that basketball is chiefly an American sport. But *le basket* is very big in France, too. Schoolchildren really like to play it, and both young and old enjoy watching the action of French professional basketball teams.

Not too long ago American players who didn't make a National Basketball Association team began playing on the newer French professional teams.

The French at Play

After a while, there were as many as three or four Americans on each team. It was finally decided to limit non-French players for a while. This way, young French players could be given a chance to play le basket in their own country.

The French invented tennis, but until recently they hadn't produced many fine players. One reason for this may be that tennis is not taught in schools or in many private clubs. You must join a tennis club or go to a special tennis camp to learn the sport.

Toto Brugnon, René Lacoste, and Henri Cochet were the last great French tennis players until a few years ago. They were famous for leading France to victory in the Davis Cup matches played between 1927 and 1932. Today, France has a great player named Yannick Noah, who is from the French West Indies. Discovered by American tennis star Arthur Ashe, Noah has become one of the top-ranked players in the world. In 1983 he won the French Open tennis championship.

Many French youngsters dream of representing their country in the Olympics one day. Over the years, France has done quite well in Olympic competition, especially in track and field events, fencing, and alpine skiing. Jean-Claude Killy won all three gold medals for alpine skiing in 1968. In 1976 Guy Drut captured the gold medal in the 110-meter hurdles.

And in 1980 the French team won four of the eight gold medals awarded for fencing.

Why are the French so good at alpine skiing? Perhaps it is because many of them grow up on the slopes of the Alps Mountains in the département of La Savoie. They have even developed their own way

France's Guy Drut won a gold medal in hurdling at the 1976 Olympic Games.

The French at Play

of skiing. This "French method" is taught throughout the world as a basic way to ski.

Fencing, or *escrime*, is a sport requiring great skill and concentration. It is very popular everywhere, but especially in Europe. And France has one of the best national fencing teams in the world.

The foil, sabre, and épée are the three types of swords used in fencing. They are only slightly different from one another in size, weight, and shape, but which one of them is used determines the rules that govern a match. These rules not only specify how the fencers may move, but also how they must touch their opponent with the sword to score points. Five touches are needed to win a match.

When the foil is used, points can only be scored by touching the trunk of the body with the sword's blunted tip. In épée fencing, any part of the body may be touched, but again only with the blunted tip of the blade. Fencers who use the sabre can score points with either the blade's tip or its cutting edges by touching any part of the body except the legs. Any of the three swords may be used in men's fencing. Only the foil may be used in women's fencing.

You may not know it, but we owe the modern Olympic Games to a Frenchman. In 1896 Baron Pierre de Coubertin announced that he had organized the Olympic Committee. Because of his efforts, the first modern Olympic Games took place that same year. He wanted countries to understand each other better and thought that their common interest in sports would be a good way to start.

That a Frenchman should have revived the Olympics is not altogether surprising. For as we have seen, the French are responsible for two of the world's most popular sports—tennis and pelota. In addition, they have long believed in the value of competition. Most of all, they have always been a playful people, enjoying everything from schoolyard tag to rough and tumble rugby.

9. From France to America

What if someone were to ask you to define American history? Would you say that it means the history of the American people, or would you explain that it refers to America's past? A teacher would probably give you credit for either answer. Yet he or she would also point out that neither is entirely correct.

One reason for this is that America is made up of so many different peoples. They have come from England, Ireland, Germany, Sweden, France, Italy, Poland, China, Korea, Japan, and many other countries. Some left their homes and families in search of adventure. Others hoped to find riches. Still others wanted the rights and freedoms America promised.

The French left home for all these reasons and more. The earliest French settlers were probably in North America as early as 1497. They were Basque, Breton, and Norman fishermen. These men would load up their ships with iron tools and kettles at home. Once here, the fishermen would trade their wares with the Indians in return for the right to fish in these people's waters. The Indians also let the Frenchmen have small plots of land. By 1510 Normandy's markets had a steady supply of codfish from

Newfoundland's shores, and France had its foothold in North America.

Later, North American furs of all sorts came into great demand in France. Beaver and otter pelts could be sold for quite a lot of money. As a result, some fishermen pulled in their nets and began setting animal traps with the help of their Indian friends.

Not all Frenchmen had good luck with the Indians they met, however. One of them was the Breton sea captain Jacques Cartier, who first explored Canada's Saint Lawrence River Valley. King Francis I of France sent Cartier to North America to find gold and other valuable metals in 1534. Some Iroquois Indians he met in the New World told him about two or three huge lakes which they said stretched to a freshwater sea. They also said the lands surrounding the lakes were brimming with gold and silver.

Cartier quickly returned to France with a few Indians to ask for help in finding these lakes. The king soon agreed since he hoped that Cartier had discovered treasure. In May 1535 he sent the explorer on a second expedition to North America.

Cartier landed on the northern coast of the Gaspé Peninsula. Then he sailed up the Saint Lawrence River to an Indian village called Hochelaga, which was located at the foot of a mountain. This mountain, which he named Mont Réal ("Mount Royal"), be-

Jacques Cartier, pictured here, was one of the earliest French explorers in North America.

came the site of the modern city of Montreal. Afterwards, he and his men sailed back to what is now Quebec City and spent the winter there. The next summer they returned to France.

Five years later Cartier made another voyage up the Saint Lawrence River. When he tried to sail on past Montreal, he was stopped by the swelling rapids of the river. He and his men then traveled on by foot, still searching for the precious metals. Finding none, they returned to a settlement near Quebec City.

Many of Cartier's men died during the long, cold, snowy winter that followed. Others were killed by Indian raiding parties who attacked the settlement in the hope of finding food. When spring came, Cartier and his entire colony packed up and went back to France.

Robert Cavelier, sieur de La Salle, a French nobleman, had more success than Cartier. He had been a fur trader at Montreal as a young man and understood the Indians and their ways. In fact, he had lived among them for many years and had even learned their language.

La Salle was certain that the Mississippi River led to the sea and that France should control the territory through which it flowed. In 1677 King Louis XIV gave him permission to explore the Mississippi to its mouth. After many hardships and failures, La Salle finally reached the Gulf of Mexico in April 1682. There he put up a cross and a column showing the French coat of arms. He also claimed all the land drained by the Mississippi and its tributaries in the name of France, calling it La Louisiane ("Louisiana") in honor of the king. This territory reached from the Appalachian Mountains on the east to the Rocky Mountains on the west, and from the Great Lakes on the north to the Gulf of Mexico on the south. Only Christopher Columbus had made a greater claim than La Salle's.

Most French people who came to North America were not adventurous nobles like La Salle. Some of them were Huguenots, who came in search of religious freedom. When Louis XIV would no longer let them practice Protestantism, as many as 400,000 Huguenots fled their country. Most of them went to England or The Netherlands since both were Protestant countries.

A number of Huguenots later traveled to North America. Many settled along the coasts of Massachusetts and New York. Over two hundred French Huguenot families arrived in New York alone between 1687 and 1688. They helped the British build their colonies and were loyal citizens.

Today many of the Huguenot's customs have disappeared. Only along the coasts of Maine do some of the old ways linger. French is widely spoken as a second language in some of Maine's cities. People say this is because Maine is so close to French-speaking Quebec, Canada. But Maine, like Louisiana, has a French heritage all its own.

The greatest number of French-speaking settlers in the United States first came from Brittany and Normandy. They were the founders of Nova Scotia. These people were called Acadians, after the French name for their land, Acadie. When the British won control of Acadie, the people remained loyal to France. They even encouraged Indians to attack English settlements. After years of wrangling between the two sides, the British decided to take a harsh course of action. Acadians who would not swear allegiance to the British king were thrown off their lands and driven out of the country. Between 6,000 and 7,500 men, women, and children were sent to English colonies farther south. Some of them ended up in Maine, while a number wandered west to Louisiana.

Acadians who went to Maine are now a very important group. They live in the Saint John Valley, which makes up Maine's northern border. Even now, French is the first language in much of the valley.

Most of the Acadians who made their way to Louisiana settled in the southern part of the state. In fact, they were the first farmers and tradespeople in the bayou area. Today quite a few of them are still farmers, but they are no longer called Acadians. Over the years they have become known as Cajuns.

The Cajuns speak French or a blend of French, Spanish, German, Indian, and Creole. In the past, the Cajuns kept to themselves, but many of them now live like their neighbors. Cajuns are particularly well known for their spicy cooking, which includes much seafood. Their traditional music, which is played by a band consisting of a fiddle, triangle, and accordion, has also received recognition.

The Cajuns are not the only French settlers to have made a lasting contribution to American life. In fact, many of the country's early leaders were originally French. And some of its revolutionary war heroes were actually French citizens.

The Marquis de Lafayette was just such a man. According to George Washington, he helped turn the tide of the Revolution and fought just like an American. When the American colonists went to war against the British, Lafayette wanted to help. He fitted his own boat and sailed for the United States at his own expense. Not long after his arrival he was made a major general in the Continental Army because of his military experience as a cavalry officer in the French army.

Everyone who met the young marquis liked him. Lafayette was a hardworking, bright, and honest man. Washington liked him so much that he put the twenty-year-old Frenchman in charge of his own forces in Virginia in 1781. His orders were to stop the British troops led by General Charles Cornwallis. Lafayette's military skill helped bring about a close to the war.

Though Lafayette returned to France after the revolutionary war was over, he never forgot the United States and its Constitution. For the next thirty years, he worked towards making the French system as strong and fair as the American one.

Pierre L'Enfant served as a major under Lafayette. He was also a gifted engineer and architect. After the close of the war, L'Enfant became an American citizen. He worked as an architect in New York until George Washington asked him to do a very special job. L'Enfant was hired to design the nation's capital in the District of Columbia.

L'Enfant met this most difficult task head-on. He decided that the focal points of the city would be Capitol Hill and the White House. After all, those places would be where all important decisions would be made. The capital would be a city of parks and history, too. Where streets met and crossed, many squares, circles, and triangles would be formed.

L'Enfant thought these places would be an ideal spot for statues or fountains.

Although L'Enfant did not carry out his plans for the city, they formed the basis for its development. He later designed Federal Hall in New York City. In 1909 a monument to him was put up in Arlington National Cemetery, where he is buried.

One of the more famous Americans of French ancestry was John James Audubon. He was the world's most famous ornithologist, or student of birds. Audubon's father had hoped his son would become a naval officer. But John James was more interested in drawing animals and birds. At the age of seventeen, he was sent to his father's estate near Philadelphia to work. Instead, Audubon continued his drawing and looking at wildlife.

Audubon traveled from Labrador, Canada, to the Gulf of Mexico searching and studying. Finally, after 1,055 paintings of different birds, Audubon published his first book, *Birds of America*. It was called an "elephant folio" because each of its pages was over three feet long and two feet wide. The book contained 435 life-sized pictures of birds, each engraved and colored by hand. Today these elephant folios are priceless.

Audubon was the first to paint birds in their natural surroundings. He was also one of the first to see nature's delicate balance. Audubon realized that all plants and animals depended on each other.

One of America's biggest success stories concerns another Frenchman and his family. Éleuthère Irénée Du Pont de Nemours and his entire family came to America about the time Napoleon Bonaparte came to power. They were French nobles and had money to invest in the new nation. At first, though, the family wasn't sure what kind of business to begin. E. I. Du Pont found the answer by accident. While hunting with a friend, his gun misfired. He soon discovered that the same thing happened about every other time if he was using American gunpowder.

Since Du Pont had studied the manufacture of gunpowder in France, he wanted to see the way Americans made it. When Du Pont saw their backward methods, he knew what kind of business his family should put its money into. The E. I. Du Pont de Nemours Company was founded, and one of America's greatest fortunes was born.

The Du Pont powder mills made gunpowder for the North during the Civil War. They also manufactured the black powder used by the pioneers who settled the American West. And they supplied the Allied Forces with explosives during World War I.

The Du Ponts did much more than make gunpowder, however. Pierre Samuel Du Pont de Nemours, E. I.'s father, was an old friend of Thomas Jefferson. He helped convince the French to sell the Louisiana Territory to the United States.

The Du Pont family owned the General Motors Corporation at one time. While it was under their management, the great French automobile engineer Louis Chevrolet sold them his car design. The Du Pont's manufacturing company made fantastic advances in the chemical industry, discovering not only nylon, but also substitutes for rubber and leather.

As you can see, then, the French have greatly contributed to America's heritage. They were the first to explore much of the territory that later became part of the United States. Their money and military power helped the colonists win independence from Great Britain. And their many inventions—margarine, canned foods, parachutes, intelligence tests, the Braille alphabet, and the stethoscope—have become familiar elements in Americans' daily lives.

The French who settled in America have also made significant contributions to its way of life. They and their descendants have played important roles in government, business, education, and the arts. Among them are Robert La Follette, Sr., a prominent Wisconsin politician and social reformer, and Jean Pierre Chouteau, who helped develop the American fur trade and settle the state of Oklahoma. His son

Pierre Chouteau, Jr., became a major figure in both the fur trade and the iron and steel business. Both the capital of South Dakota, Pierre, and Chouteau, Montana, were named in his honor. High honors have also been paid to Thomas Hopkins Gallaudet, a pioneer in the education of deaf people, and to John La Farge, often called "the father of mural painting in America."

You may not recall many of these names in the years to come. But there is one way you can remember what France and its people have meant to America. Just think of the Statue of Liberty. Given to the United States by France in 1884, this famous monument symbolizes the friendship between the two countries as well as the freedoms they both so greatly cherish.

Appendix A

French Consulates in the United States and Canada

The French consulates in the United States and Canada want to help North Americans understand French ways. For more information about France, contact the consulate or embassy nearest you.

U. S. Consulates

Boston, Massachusetts
French Consulate General
3 Commonwealth Avenue
Boston, Massachusetts 02116
Phone (617) 266-1680

Chicago, Illinois
French Consulate General
919 North Michigan Avenue
Chicago, Illinois 60611
Phone (312) 263-6067

Detroit, Michigan
French Consulate General
1938 National Bank Building
Detroit, Michigan 48226
Phone (313) 963-0553

Houston, Texas
French Consulate General
920 Esperson Building
Houston, Texas 77002
Phone (713) 228-0218

Los Angeles, California
French Consulate General
9255 Sunset Boulevard
Los Angeles, California 90069
Phone (213) 272-5452

New Orleans, Louisiana
French Consulate General
3305 Saint Charles Avenue
New Orleans, Louisiana 70115
Phone (504) 897-6381

New York, New York
French Consulate General
934 Fifth Avenue
New York, New York 10021
Phone (212) 535-0100

San Francisco, California
French Consulate General
2570 Jackson Street
San Francisco, California 94115
Phone (415) 922-3255

Washington, D.C.
Embassy of France
2535 Belmont Road NW
Washington, D.C. 20008
Phone (202) 234-0990

French Consulate General
2129 Wyoming Avenue NW
Washington, D.C. 20008
Phone (202) 322-8400

Canadian Consulates

Montreal, Quebec
    French Consulate General
    2 Elysée (Floor E) Place Bonaventure
    Montreal, Quebec
    Phone (514) 878-4381

Ottawa, Ontario
    Embassy of France
    42 Sussex Drive
    Ottawa, Ontario K1M 2C9
    Phone (613) 232-1795

Quebec, Quebec
    French Consulate General
    1110 Avenue des Laurentides
    Quebec, Quebec G1S 3C3
    Phone (418) 688-0430

Toronto, Ontario
    French Consulate General
    40 University Avenue, Suite 620
    Toronto, Ontario M9J 1T1
    Phone (416) 366-1131

Vancouver, British Columbia
    French Consulate General
    Suite 1201, The Vancouver Block
    736 Granville Street
    Vancouver, British Columbia V6Z 1H9
    Phone (604) 681-2301

Appendix B

A Note About Pronouncing French Words

French is the official language of France. It is also one of the official languages of Belgium, Canada, Luxembourg, Switzerland, and the United Nations. More than 80 million people speak French as their first language, and millions of others use it as a second one.

English-speaking people often find French words difficult to say, however. One reason for this is that the final consonants in French words are rarely pronounced, excepting, in most cases, the letters *c, f, l,* and *r*. *Lits* ("beds"), for example, is said as if it were spelled *lee*. In addition, syllables ending in *n* or *m*, such as in *bon* ("good"), have a very nasal sound to them.

Vowels can also present a problem. Some, such as the *i* sound in *bise* ("north wind"), are shorter than the English sound—in this case *bees*—that most closely approximates them. Others, such as the *u* sound in *lune* ("moon"), have no equivalent in English. To pronounce this *u* you must round your lips as if you're going to whistle and then try to say the *e* sound of *he*.

One day you may want to learn more about speaking French. For now, though, you may want to try saying the words and expressions that follow.

après (ah PREH)—after
au revoir (oh ruh VWAHR)—good-bye
blanc (blawng)—white
bleu (bluhr)—blue
bonjour (bohng JHOOR)—hello
chose (shohz)—thing
dans (dawng)—in, into
de (duh)—of, from
enfant (awng FAWNG)—child
frère (frair)—brother
garçon (GAHR sohng)—boy; waiter
joli (johl EE)—pretty
maison (may ZOHNG)—house
mauvais (moh VAY)—bad
mère (mair)—mother
père (pair)—father
pour (poor)—for
quatre (kah truh)—four
rouge (roozh)—red
sans (sawng)—without
très bien (treh BYANG)—very well

Glossary

Acadie (AH kah dee)—Acadia; now called Nova Scotia

appellation d'origine contrôlée (AH pehl ah see ohng DAWR ee jheeng KOHNG troh lay)—Controlled Place of Origin; laws that govern the bottling and labeling of French wines

baccalauréat (BAK ah lohr AY ah)—the diploma awarded to French students who complete high school and pass a special examination

baguette (bah GEHT)—a long loaf of French sourdough bread

(le) basket (luh BASK eht)—basketball

bassin de Paris (BAH sang duh pah REE)—the Parisian Basin, France's central region

(La) Bastille (lah BAHS tee)—a Parisian fortress where French kings kept political prisoners

B. E. C. (bay eh say)—the diploma awarded to French students when they complete junior high school

B. E. P. (bay eh pay)—the general professional diploma awarded by French vocational high schools

(le) bocage (luh boh KAHJHAH)—the wooded area of Brittany
bois de Boulogne (bwah duh BOO lohng)—the Boulogne woods, a forest in Paris
bon appétit (bohng ah pay tee)—happy eating
Bonjour, Messieurs, Dames (bohng JHOOR MAY see yuh DAHM)—Hello, ladies and gentlemen
bonne année (buhn an NAY)—Happy New Year
boulangerie (BOO lawng juhur ee)—a bread shop
brevet de Technicien (breh vay duh TEHK nee see ihng)—the technical diploma awarded to students who complete high school and pass a special examination
bûche de Noël (boosh duh noh el)—Yule log pastry
café (kah fay)—an informal bar and restaurant
café au lait (kah FAY oh LAY)—coffee with warm milk
Cajuns (KAH jhung)—descendants of the Acadians who settled in Louisiana
C. A. P. (say ah pay)—a specialized diploma awarded by French vocational high schools
caves (kahv)—wine cellars
Certificat de Fin d'Etudes Secondaires (SAIR tee fee kah duh fing DEE tood SEH gowng dair)—the

certificate which is awarded to French students who complete high school
chalets (sha LAY)—cottages
(la) Chandeleur (lah SHAWND lur)—Candelmas, the festival celebrated on February 2
châteaux (shah TOH)—refers both to castles and to huge family estates
(le) chèvre d'or (leh SHEVRUH dawr)—the golden-fleeced goat
Code Napoléon (kahd NAH poh LAY ohng)—a strict set of laws concerning property and the family that were issued by Napoleon Bonaparte
coiffes (KWAHF)—lacy headdresses that are part of the folk costumes worn by women in Brittany
collège (koh lehjh)—junior high school
(le) complément familial (luh kahm PLAY mang FAH mee lee ahl)—money the French government gives to citizens with large families
C. P. A. (say pay ah)—a school program for apprenticeship in a trade
crêpes (krehp)—thin pancakes
croissants (KRAWH sang)—crescent rolls
croque monsieur (krohk muh SEEYUH)—a ham and cheese sandwich

cycle d'observation (see kehl DAHB sur VAH see ohng)—the first two years of junior high school
cycle d'orientation (see kehl DAWR ee n TAH see ohng)—the second two years of junior high school
déjeuner (DAY jhun AY)—lunch
département (DAY pahr teh mawng)—a French administrative unit
(le) drac (leh drak)—the tiny being in French folktales who is said to like horses
émir (AY meer)—an Arab ruler
épée (ay pay)—a fencing sword with a rigid, three-sided blade and a round hand guard
(L') Equipe de France (LAY KEEP duh frawns)—the French National Team
escrime (EHS kreem)—fencing
(les) étrennes (lays AY trehn)—the gifts the French give their friends on New Year's Day
fête de la vigne (feht duh lah VEENG)—a wine festival
(les) feux de Saint Jean (lay fuh duh sang jhang)—Saint John's bonfires, a rural festival that celebrates midsummer
foil (foyl)—a fencing sword with a four-sided blade and a round hand guard

(La) foire au Jambon (lah fwarh oh JAHNG bohng)—the Ham Feast celebrated at Eastertime; the oldest food festival in France
(le) football (luh FOOT bawl)—soccer
(les) footballeurs (lay foot BAWL uhr)—soccer players
franglais (FRAWN glay)—a form of slang that consists of a mixture of French and English words
(le) fronton (luh FROHNG tong)—the backboard wall used in pelota
galette des rois (gah LEHT day rwah)—a large, round, puffy pastry containing a single bean; it is baked on Epiphany
gendarmes (jhawng DAHRM)—French police
grand chef de cuisine (gran shehf duh kwee zeen)—a great chef
(le) gros poisson (leh groh PWAH sohng)—the great fish
guignol (GEENG nahl)—French puppet theater
hôtels particuliers (oh tehl pahr TEE koo lee ay)—large, old private homes
huitieme (wee TEE ehm)—the eighth grade in French schools; equivalent to fourth grade in American schools

(le) jeu de paume (luh jhuh duh pawm)—the earliest version of tennis
koligan (koh LEE gawng)—the mischievous dwarves of Carnac
L. E. G. T. (el eh jay tay)—a general high school
L. E. P. (el eh pay)—a vocational high school
lycée (lee SAY)—high school
maillot jaune (MY oh jhohng)—a yellow T-shirt worn by the overall winner of the Tour de France
Mardi Gras (mahr DEE grah)—Fat Tuesday, the day before Ash Wednesday; also known as Shrove Tuesday
Marseillais (mahr SAY yay)—a person from the city of Marseille
(la) masquérade du Cherubim (lah mahs kehr ahd doo SHAYR oo bang)—the cherub's masquerade, an early version of Halloween
ondines (awn DEEN)—water fairies
onzième (owng ZEE ehm)—the eleventh grade in French schools; equivalent to first grade in American schools
pardons (pahr DOHNG)—the yearly pilgrimage the people of Brittany make to a saint's tomb
par excellence (pahr EHX say lawngs)—superb

pâtisserie (PAH tees uhr ee)—a bakery
pâtisseries (PAH tees uhr ee)—pastries
(la) pelote (lah PAY loht)—the ball used to play pelota
(la) pelote Basque (lah PAY loht bask)—Basque pelota
(le) père fouettard (luh pair foo eht TAHR)—the Whip Father, the figure said to punish bad children at Christmastime
(le) père Noël (luh pair noh el)—Santa Claus
(le) petit déjeuner (luh peh TEE DAY jhun AY)—breakfast
(les) petits hommes cornus (lay peh TEES uhm KAWR noo)—the little horned men who are told about in French folktales; they are said to keep a tremendous fortune in gold
poisson d'avril (PWAH sohng dav reel)—April Fools' Day
(la) politesse (lah POH LEE tehs)—a code of proper behavior
portes cochères (pohrt KOH shayr)—courtyard doors
(les) quatre heures (lay KAH truh uhr)—"the four o'clocks"; teatime
quiche (keezh)—a cheese and egg pie

réveillon (ray VAY yohng)—an elaborate meal eaten on Christmas Eve and New Year's Eve

(le) roi soleil (luh rwah SOH lay)—the Sun King, the name given to Louis XIV

sabre (sahbr)—a fencing sword with a flat, thin blade and a curving hand guard

santons (SAHN tawng)—little saint figurines that are made at Christmastime

sapin de Noël (SA pang duh noh el)—a Christmas tree

septième (seh TEE ehm)—the seventh grade in French schools; equivalent to fifth grade in American schools

solèves (SOH lehv)—garden elves who are said to live in the French Alps

terminal (TAIR mee nal)—the last year of high school

territoires d'Outre-Mer (TER REE toyr DOO trawr MAIR)—the Overseas Territories, lands in the South Pacific Ocean, Africa, Latin America, and the Caribbean Sea that are governed by France

tirer le roi (tih RAY leh rwah)—"draw out the king"; to find the bean in the Epiphany pastry

Tour de France (tuhr duh frawns)—a bicycle race that takes place in France each year

trait d'union (treh DUHN ee ohng)—a hyphen

troubadours (troo BAH dawr)—traveling singers/songwriters who told stories about the times in which they lived
tu (too)—the familiar word for *you*; used only when one is speaking to family members or close friends
un petit café (oon peh TEE kah FAY)—a bit of coffee
vendange (vawng DAWNGE)—the grape harvest
vieilles dames (vee ay DAHM)—elderly women
villas (vee lah)—newer private homes
vous (voo)—the polite word for *you*; used when one is speaking to strangers or acquaintances

Selected Bibliography

Books for Younger Readers

Carroll, Joseph T. *The French: How They Live and Work*. New York: Praeger Publishers, 1970.

Edwards, Harvey. *France and the French*. Nashville, Tennessee: Thomas Nelson, 1972.

Ellis, D. L. *Life in a French Family*. London: Harrap, 1968.

———. *Life in a French Town*. London: Harrap, 1973.

Froment-Meurice, F., and Dandelot, M. *France*. (English version). Paris: La Documentation Française, 1975.*

Holbrook, Sabra. *France: The Invisible Revolution*. Nashville, Tennessee: Thomas Nelson, 1973.

———. *Growing up in France*. New York: Atheneum Press, 1980.

Pien, Tomiche. *The French and the Nation*. Paris: La Documentation Française, 1980.*

*Note: Title may be obtained through local French consulate libraries at little or no cost.

Index

agriculture, French, 12, 16-17
Alps, 10, 12, 110
Appert, Nicolas, 54
Audubon, John James, 121-122
baccalauréat, 98
baguette, 21, 86
Basques: eating contests of, 27; explorers and, 26; games of, 26-27; in North America, 113-114; origins of, 24-25; shepherds and, 26
bassin de Paris, 10
(La) Bastille, 50
Bismarck, Otto von, 56
(le) bocage, 9
bois de Boulogne, 13
Bonaparte, Louis Napoleon, 55-56
Bonaparte, Napoleon, 53-55
bon appétit, 88
bonne année, 69
boulangerie, 34, 85
Bretons, 22-23, 113-114
Brevet de Technicien, 98
Brevet d'Etudes des Collèges, 97
Brevet d'Etude Professionel, 100
Brittany, 9-10, 22-24
bûche de Noël, 73-74
Caesar, Julius, ancient France and, 37
café au lait, 30
Carnac, 24
Cartier, Jacques, North American explorations of, 114-116
caves, 32
celebrations, French: All Saints' Day, 76; *la Chandeleur* (Candlemas), 69-71; Christmas, 72-75; Easter, 72; Epiphany, 69; *La foire au Jambon*, 76; *la masquérade du Cherubim*, 76; New Year's Day, 68-69; *poisson d'avril* (April Fools' Day), 72; Saint Catherine's Day, 68; Saint John's Day, 75; Shrove Tuesday (Mardi Gras), 71-72
Certificat d'Aptitude Professionelle, 100
Certificat de Fin d'Etudes Secondaires, 100
chalets, 78
Charlemagne, empire of, 37-38
Charles VII, King, 42
Charles the Bald, King, 38
châteaux, 32, 78
(la) chèvre d'or, 60
children, French: grandparents and, 85-86; helping at home of, 85; rights of, 82-83
Chouteau, Jean Pierre, 123
Chouteau, Pierre, Jr., 124
cities, French, 14-16
city life, French, 79-82
Code Napoléon, 55
coiffes, 23
Common Market, European, 57
(le) complément familial, 83-85
Cours préparatoires a l'apprentissage, 96
crêpes, flipping of at Candlemas, 71
croissants, 86
cycle d'observation, 96
cycle d'orientation, 97

Declaration of the Rights of Man and the Citizen, 51
de Coubertin, Baron Pierre, 111
de Gaulle, General Charles, 57-58
déjeuner, 87
départements, 54-55
d'Estaing, Valéry Giscard, 58
Dictionnaire de la Cuisine, 88
drac, 62-63
drivers, French, 29
Drut, Guy, 109
duke of Burgundy, 44
Dumas, Alexandre, 88
Du Pont family, 122-123
Edict of Nantes, 49
Eleanor of Aquitaine, 39-40
épée, 111
(les) étrennes, 69
farm life, French, 82
fashion, French, 13
fête de la vigne, 32
(les) feux de la Saint Jean, 75
folktales, French: Genèsi and *le gros poisson*, 61-62; Janet and the golden goat, 60-61; *koligans*, 63; about the Moors, 59-60; about the mysterious *drac*, 62-63; *les petits hommes cornus*, 65
foods, French: at breakfast, 30, 86; cheeses, 32-34; at dinner, 30; at "four o'clocks," 87-88; at lunch, 30, 85, 87; market days and, 34-35; pleasures of, 30; shopping for, 34; wines, 30-32
Fos-sur-Mer, 17-18
franglais, 28
Franks, tribe of, 37
(le) fronton, 107

(la) galette des rois, 69
Gallaudet, Thomas Hopkins, 124
Gauls, tribe of, 37
gendarmes, shaking hands of, 29
geography, French, 7-12
government, French, 20, 82-83
grand chef de cuisine, 88
guignol, 104
Henry IV, King, 44-46
Henry V, King, 40
holidays. *See* celebrations, French
hôtels particuliers, 78
houses, French: furniture of, 79; kitchens of, 79; windows of, 78
Huguenots, 46-47, 49, 117-118
Hundred Years' War, 42
immigrants, French: Acadians, 118-119; achievements of, 120-124; Huguenots, 117-118; reasons for immigration of, 113-114; settlements of, 113-118
industrial planning, French, 18-20
Industrial Revolution, 56
international road signs, 16
Joan of Arc, 40-44
Killy, Jean-Claude, 109
koligans, 63
La Farge, John, 124
Lafayette, Marquis de, in American Revolution, 119-120
La Follette, Robert, Sr., 123
Lancelot du Lac, Sir, 24
language, French: English words and, 27-28; polite usage of, 28-29; worldwide use of, 27
La Salle, North American explorations of, 116-117

le Fay, Morgan, 24
legends, French, King Richard I in, 65-66
L'Enfant, Pierre, 120-121
Les Camargues, 12
Les Landes, 10
Lille, industries of, 9
Louis VII, King, 39-40
Louis XI, King, 44
Louis XIII, King, 46
Louis XIV, King, 47-49
Louis XVI, King, 49-51
Louisiana: Acadian settlers in, 118-119; Cajun customs of, 119; naming of, 117
Lycée d'Enseignement Général et Technologique, 98
Lycée d'Enseignement Professionel, 100
maillot jaune, 108
Maine, Huguenots and Acadians in, 117-118
Marie Antoinette, 49, 51
Marseillais, 61
middle class, French, 50
Mississippi River, exploration of, 116-117
Mitterand, François, 58
Montreal, founding of, 114-116
Noah, Yannick, 109
nobles, French, 39-40, 50-51, 55
Normandy, 9
ondines, 59
pardons, 23
Paris, 13
Parliament, French, 20
pâtisserie, 34
pâtisseries, 87-88
peasants, French, 49-50

pelote, 27, 107
(le) père fouettard, 74
(le) père Noël, 74
Pétain, Marshal Henri Philippe, 56-57
(un) petit café, 86
(le) petit déjeuner, 86
(la) politesse, 28-29
Pompidou, Georges, 58
portes cochères, 78
puppets, French, 104
Pyrénées Mountains, 10, 12
Pyrénées, province of, 24
Quebec City, 116
recipes: Crêpes, 89; Croque Monsieur, 90; Three Cheese Quiche, 90-91
Reign of Terror, 51
réveillon, 68-69
Revolution, French, 50-53
Richelieu, Cardinal, 46-47
Roquefort cheese, 34
sabre, 111
Saint Lawrence River, 114-116
santons, 74
sapin de Noël, 72-73
sayings, French, 66-67
schools, French: *collège*, 96-98; daily schedule of, 92; elementary, 95-96; history of, 92; *lycées*, 98-101; nursery, 94-95; private, 101; subjects in, 93-94, 96-97
solèves, 59
southern France, 10-12
sports, French: *le basket* (basketball), 108-109; cycling, 108; *escrime* (fencing), 111; *le football* (soccer), 105-106; *le jeu de paume* (palm ball), 102; Olympic Games and, 109-112; pelota, 107;

school training for, 104-105; skiing, 110-111; tennis, 102-103, 109
States-General, 50
Statue of Liberty, 124
terminal, 100
territoires d'Outre Mer, 7
tirer le roi, 69
town life, French, 82
trait d'union, 21-22
Treaty of Troyes, 40
troubadours, 37, 40
truffles, pigs and, 13
TV, French, 86
vendange, 32
Verne, Jules, Brittany and, 24
villas, 78
Waterloo, defeat of Napoleon at, 55
work schedules, French, 85

The photographs are reproduced through the courtesy of Susan Balerdi, George Hulstrand, Air France, Food and Wines from France, the French Cultural Service, and the French Government Tourist Office. The cover photograph and the pictures on pages 84, 93, 94, 95, 97, 103, 104, and 107 were supplied by Jeanine Landau.

About the Author

France is sometimes pictured as a country where people eat camembert cheese, drink wine, wear berets, and ride bicycles. But Susan Balerdi wants young people to know that "France is as varied in its history, culture, and geography as the United States." Moreover, she wants them to understand that the French "are just as proud of their heritage as Americans are of theirs."

Ms. Balerdi is well qualified to speak about France and its people. As a college student, she attended the Université de Dijon, where she completed a self-designed study program in French political science and economics. Afterwards she continued to live and work in France for five years. This experience eventually helped her become the corporate secretary and treasurer for a French hotel chain in North America.

Now a children's writer and a free-lance commercial artist living in White Plains, New York, Ms. Balerdi remains a Francophile. She and her husband—a Frenchman—speak only French at home. In addition, they frequently talk about France with their three children—Matti, Zandy, and Andrew.

j944 B28f   WES
Balerdi, Susan
France, the crossroads of
  Europe   1000

This book has been withdrawn from the St. Joseph County Public Library due to

___ deteriorated/defective condition
___ obsolete information
___ superceded by newer holdings
✓ excess copies/reduced demand
___ other _____

_____
    Date   Staff

NOV. 1 5 1984